CONTROVERSIAL TOPICS AMONGST BELIEVERS OF THE BIBLE

TONIDA J. COOPER

PREFACE

I thank Father Yah for giving me revelation and for the horrible experience to write this book. This book is personal to me because of the terror I went through regarding this matter. I hope this gives readers a better understanding of each topic. Please research for yourself.

Shalom

TABLE OF CONTENT

INTRODUCTION

Greetings to all that is taking the time to read this book. It is a short book to quickly reference hot topics that are often controversial amongst believers because the scriptures are often misinterpreted. Much of what is taught in some churches (**not all**) keeps people in bondage. This book will help to clear the confusion. I am not saying I have the knowledge of all but I have studied and researched well because of several topics in this book, I was delivered from bondage when Yah opened my eyes, and I had to unlearn what was taught to me. All glory is to Yahuah. HalleluYah!

Throughout the book, I will be using the Hebrew names of Yah and his son Yahshua whom most of you call God/Lord and Jesus. Please also see my book regarding the true name of our creator.

CHAPTER I
SPEAKING IN TONGUES IS A GIFT
This does not necessarily mean that you are reborn and filled with the Holy Spirit by speaking in tongues

This is mostly pushed by leaders from Pentecostal and Apostolic churches abruptly and sharply. Teaching that unless one receives the gift of an unknown tongue is not filled with the Holy Spirit (**Ruach Ha Quodesh**), is simply incorrect. The scripture they love to misinterpret is **Acts 2:1-3 (below), regarding the day of Pentecost**. This scripture has been misunderstood for a while to be wrongly used as evidence that individuals are not filled or reborn by the Holy Spirit unless they speak in an unknown tongue. The apostles received the gift of an unknown tongue first because they were waiting for what Yahshua promised. However, the Holy Spirit supernaturally gave them the interpretation of what each other was saying in the different languages they spoke. Gentiles that spoke different languages outside of Hebrew could understand what they were saying because each apostle was speaking a language other than Hebrew. Giving a message that the comforter will guide all into full truth with the mighty works of Yah. once they accept Yahshua the Messiyah. This is the reason that the apostles spoke different languages. Scripture points out that Yah-fearing men from every nation that heard the rushing when gathered together to listen and were amazed that each nation of people could understand what the apostles were saying in each of their languages about the mighty works of Yah (**Acts 2:5-12**). Therefore, if one receives the gift of tongues it is simply one of the gifts listed in **1 Corinthians**. It is an unknown tongue to the individual that received it, however, Apostle Paul makes a valid point that if anyone receives the gift of an unknown tongue to also pray for the interpretation of the unknown language. This way the individual can share it with the assembly. Otherwise, the individual speaking the unknown language is the only one being edified in their spirit although they cannot understand the language either.

If there, were a chance of getting your prayers to Yah when you do not know what to pray for by praying in an unknown language then I believe that Yah would have made it so everyone would receive an unknown tongue. Scripture says that Yah will withhold no good thing from His people. Nevertheless, if that was the case it is a good thing, and we all would have received the gift of an unknown language because sometimes life can get so hard or one can experience such trauma, or fall so hard that they cannot even pray for themselves. Therefore, if praying in another language would help that individual get his or her prayers to Yah in definite, do you not think that Yah would grant everyone that gift. It does not make sense not to if that were the case knowing that Yah is no respect of persons (**Romans 2:11**) to only allow some individuals to receive this gift and not all. Yah wills that no one should perish (**2 Peter 3:9**) However, there is a solution to that. It is written in the laws of Yah, **Romans 8:26-27** that when individuals are too weak and in despair not knowing what to pray for the Holy Spirit will intercede on their behalf. The law did not say when individuals speak in an unknown tongue the spirit will then intervene. It did not say when individuals get to the point of not being able to pray for themselves they will start speaking in an unknown tongue and the spirit will intercede for them. According to the law of Yah, no one is more special than the other. However, some Christians that have received this gift of an unknown language are guilty of self-righteous judgment by looking at individuals that have not received the gift of an unknown language. They are guilty of placing **THEMSELVES** on a paddle stool by thinking they are above those that have not received the gift of an unknown language. Therefore, the gift of an unknown language is over-emphasized. According to Apostle Paul, the gift of an unknown language is not as important as the other gifts because it gives self-edification to that individual "**only**" but not the whole assembly. He stated that if anyone desires to speak in an unknown language also pray for the interpretation of the unknown language. This is also, why it is out of order for more than two people to be speaking an unknown language in the assembly unless there is an interpreter. Because the assembly is the spiritual body and each member, makes up the body part using the gifts to perfect the body. If everyone is speaking in an unknown language then how can the spiritual body understand what Yah is saying to the assembly?

This is why Apostle Paul, emphasizes that he rather a Prophet speak five words to the assembly so that everyone can understand, verses someone speaking an unknown tongue of a thousand words because it does not edify the full body but only the individual which makes sense.

What about being reborn of the spirit and the fruits of the SPIRIT that are evidence that one is reborn. If one speaks in an unknown tongue but has not changed their sinful lifestyle by being reborn of the spirit is a big problem because when one allows the Holy Spirit to take over their lives by leading them into all truth spiritually, they become reborn of the spirit, however, the individual might not have ever spoke tongues but they are filled with the Holy Spirit. Yes, speaking in an unknown tongue is one of the ways of knowing one is filled with the spirit but being reborn of the spirit and seeing the fruit it bears is when one is filled with the Holy Spirit. Do you know that the individual speaking in an unknown tongue can have no fruit but the one that does not speak in an unknown tongue can bear fruit?

When the day of Pentecost had come, all of Yahshua's taught ones were all together in one place. Suddenly a sound came from heaven like a violent rushing wind. It filled the whole house where they were sitting. There appeared to them tongues resembling fire, which was being distributed [**among them**]. The different languages rested on each of them [**as each person received the Holy Spirit**]. And they were all filled [**that is, diffused throughout their being**] with the Holy Spirit and began to speak in other tongues (**different languages**), as the Spirit was giving them the ability to speak out [**clearly and appropriately**]. Although the tongues they spoke were separate languages, they could understand each other through the power of the Holy Spirit. Evidence that the tongues are different languages because the other nations heard them speaking their language, and each could understand what was said. **See the scripture below as proof.**

Acts 2:5-12

Now, there were Judeans (Yah's chosen better known today as Israelites) living in Jerusalem, devout and **Yah-fearing men from every nation under heaven**. And when this sound was heard, a crowd gathered, and **they were bewildered because each one was hearing those in the upper room speaking in his language *or* dialect**. They were utterly astonished, saying, "Look! Are not all of these who are speaking Galileans? Then, how is it that each of us hears in our language or native dialect? [**Among us there are**] Parthians, Medes, and Elamites, and people of Mesopotamia, Judea and Cappadocia, Pontus and Asia [**Minor**], Phrygia and Pamphylia, Egypt and the districts of Libya around Cyrene, and the visitors from Rome, both Judeans and proselytes (**Gentile converts to Judaism**), Cretans and Arabs—we all hear them speaking in our [**native**] language about the mighty works of Yah!" And they were beside themselves with amazement and were greatly perplexed, saying one to another, "They are full of sweet wine and are drunk!"

For example: If the assembly had service and a foreigner walked into the church but does not speak the language of those in the assembly. One may start speaking in an unknown tongue (**of the foreigner**) to be able to translate what is being said.

1 Corinthians 14:20-25 (Apostle Paul Speaking)

Brothers and sisters, do not be children [**immature, childlike**] in your thinking; be infants in [**matters of**] evil [**completely innocent and inexperienced**], but in your minds be mature [**adults**]. It is written in the Law, "BY MEN OF STRANGE TONGUES AND BY THE LIPS OF FOREIGNERS I WILL SPEAK TO THIS PEOPLE, AND NOT EVEN THEN WILL THEY LISTEN TO ME," says Yah (**Isaiah 28:11**). Therefore, [**unknown**] tongues are [**meant**] for a [**supernatural**] sign, not to believers but to unbelievers [**who might be receptive**]; while prophecy [**foretelling the future, speaking a new message from Yah to the people**] is not for unbelievers but believers. So then, if the whole church gathers together and all of you speak in [**unknown**] tongues, and outsiders, or those who are not gifted [**in spiritual matters**] or unbelievers come in, will they not say that you are out of your mind? But if all prophecy [**foretelling the future, speaking a new message from Yah to the people**], and an unbeliever or outsider comes in, he is convicted [**of his sins**] by all, and he is called to account by all [**because he can understand what is being said**]; the secrets of his heart are laid bare. And so, falling on his face, he will worship Yah, declaring that Yah is really among you.

Commentary: This scripture above breaks down further what the gifts of tongues are used for. The gifts of tongues are a supernatural sign that Yah is real and speaks to his people about the ways of life he wants them to live. The believers (**the Judeans**) believe. However, the unknown tongues are for outsiders that are not believers or have not been gifted spiritually. It has nothing to do with them being filled with the Holy Spirit as evidence.

Please see the breakdown below with scripture backup that many churches teach what the meaning of tongues is in error. Yah has given me a clear understanding of the true meaning of being filled with the holy spirit, and it is as follows:

MEANING OF PENTECOST: A festival celebration of when the Holy Spirit descended from heaven on the disciples of Yahshua after his Ascension returning back to the Father in Heaven, held on the seventh day.

Pentecost took place one time **only**. That was **when the believers (Yahshua's taught ones) were waiting for the comforter as he promised,** once He Ascended back to heaven with Yah. Just as He promised, the helper descended upon his taught ones that day. And any other that will follow the teachings of Yahshua and build a relationship to help guide them. Suddenly a sound came from heaven like a violent rushing wind, and it filled the whole house where Yahshua's disciples were. There appeared to them tongues resembling fire (**spreading like wildfire**) which was distributed (**among them**). Tongues rested on **each one of them (as each anticipated and received the Holy Spirit**), they were all filled with the Fruits of the Holy Spirit and continued to do what Yahshua was doing on earth **with power** as He promised, **even more, significant than Yahshua told them their works will be** while being led into all truth through the Holy Spirit that was promised to them. **So t**hey received the gift of tongues (**different languages**) and were **filled with the fruits of the spirit too.**

The **gift** of tongues is different from being **filled** with the Holy Spirit. **THE GIFT OF THE TONGUE IS DIFFERENT LANGUAGES.** Matthew 3:8-10 (The Fruits of the Spirit is evidence when people are filled with the fruits of the spirit), **please see the breakdown below.**

So produce **FRUIT THAT IS CONSISTENT WITH REPENTANCE [demonstrating new behavior that proves a change of heart, and conscious decisions to turn away from sin]**, and do not presume to say to yourselves [**as a defense**]. 'We have Abraham for our father [**so our inheritance assures us of salvation**]'; for I say to you that from these stones YAH can raise children (**descendants**) for Abraham. And already the ax [**of YAH's judgment**] is swinging toward the root of the trees; **therefore, every tree that does not bear good fruit is cut down and thrown**

into the fire. FRUITS OF THE SPIRIT: *love [unselfish concern for others], joy, [inner] peace, patience [not the ability to wait, but how we act while waiting], kindness, goodness, faithfulness, gentleness, self-control.* **The fruit of the spirit is the Ruach Ha Quadesh (Holy Spirit), sent as a comforter to lead us in all truth. Therefore when one is filled with it. The Fruits of the spirit will be evident in the walk of the believer.**

Many individuals speak with the gift of tongues that does not bear fruit nor carry any of the characteristics of the fruits of the spirit. **Therefore they are not filled with the Holy Spirit**. I have witnessed people in the church that speak with the gift of tongues and were as evil as demons. Therefore they were not bearing fruits as evidence that the Holy Spirit dwells within. Do not let anyone fool you into thinking because they speak in an unknown language, aka "the gift of tongues," that they are filled with the Holy Spirit **when** they are not bearing fruits of the Spirit. Yahshua said that you will know them by their fruits (**Matthew 7:16-18**). *Every good tree brings forth good fruit, but a corrupt tree brings forth evil fruit. A good tree cannot bring forth evil fruit, neither can a corrupt tree bring forth good fruit. Without the fruits of the spirit, no one is filled with the Holy Spirit. The unknown tongue is a gift that one receives, and gifts are given without repentance, according to* **Romans 11:29.**
People that believe in Yah through His son Yahshua can use any gift given to them and not be filled with the Holy Spirit. I will provide a few examples. For instance, some may have the gift of healing and heal many people from various things to get the glory for themselves, but not to glorify Father Yah. Some may have the gift of knowledge by understanding the laws of Yah with no lack of understanding. They can read something and immediately as they read the laws of Yah, they understand it. But not necessarily filled with the Holy

Spirit but filled with knowledge. One can have the gift of teaching. Share their knowledge with the body of Yahshua (**the assembly**) very clearly, and people will understand with no problem. However, they may not be filled with the Holy Spirit. Their gift of teaching magnifies so well that they can make a baby understand what they are teaching. Yahshua said, on judgment day, many will say, have I not cast out devils in your name? Have I not taught in your name? Have I not prophesied in your name etc. Then he will say depart from me, you worker of iniquity, I never knew you.

Think about it, would Yahshua say that if you were filled with the Holy Spirit, you would speak in another language? He said that I would send a helper. "The Holy Spirit" is whom He sent to help guide you into all truth. As one walks into all truth, they start bearing fruits, which are the gifts of the fruits of the spirit. One can still operate in their gift and not be filled with the Holy Spirit because gifts come without repentance. When one repents, they turn from their sinful and wicked ways and follow the laws and commands of Yah, which brings them nigh to Yah in a relationship. As the Holy Spirit leads into all truth, it goes hand and hand. **See the breakdown of scripture below.**

A Tree and Its Fruit
"Beware of the false prophets, [**teachers**] who come to you dressed as sheep [**appearing gentle and innocent**], but inwardly are ravenous wolves. By their fruit, you will recognize them [**that is, by their contrived doctrine and self-focus**]. Do people pick grapes from thornbushes or figs from

thistles? Even so, every healthy tree bears good fruit, but the unhealthy tree bears bad fruit. A good tree cannot bear bad fruit, nor can a bad tree bear good fruit. Every tree that does not bear good fruit is cut down and thrown into the fire. Therefore, by their fruit, you will recognize them [**as false prophets**].[21] "Not everyone who says to Me, Adonai, Adonai,' will enter the kingdom of heaven, but only he who does the will of My Father who is in heaven. [22] Many will say to Me on that day [**when I judge them**], Adonai, Adonai, have we not prophesied in Your name, and driven out demons in Your name, and done many miracles in Your name?' And then I will declare to them publicly, 'I never knew you; DEPART FROM ME [**you are banished from My presence**], YOU WHO ACT WICKEDLY [**disregarding My commands**].' A believer being filled with the Holy Spirit does not disregard the commands of Yah.

According to **John 15:26,** the helper (**Holy Spirit**) was sent to help guide Yahshua's followers into all truth when He ascended back to heaven to be with the Father. The Helper leads all followers into all truth. Therefore, he continued to do the same for the disciples as they continued in the teachings of Yahshua. Yahshua taught them for years, and they followed his ways and became like Him. Finally, the Holy Spirit descended on them, and they were filled with the fruits of the Spirit. It takes time to bear fruits because once one has decided to follow Yahshua, the fruits of the spirits will come. However, spiritual gifts can come without repentance and be given immediately. Some are born with their gifts. For example, the gift of teaching might have always been evident in someone since they were a child. The way they speak to individuals is to explain things to them and they get it immediately. When one receives the gift of an unknown tongue. In that case, it is usually given after one becomes a believer in the laws of Yah.

However, if one is born with this gift, it does not manifest until one confesses to Yahshua and starts studying the scriptures. Each assembly member is given a gift, and one can pray for a particular gift too. The Holy Spirit gives gifts. This is why some people can be no more than two months in the truth and get immersed (**baptized**) and come up out of the water speaking in an unknown tongue. They were given the gift of an unknown language, but that does not mean that they are filled with the Holy Spirit. One has to start out with milk as a babe in Yahshua, as one becomes obedient and grows from milk to the maturity of meat (**1 Corinthians 3:2-3**). Then the fruits of the Spirit manifest, and they will be filled with the Holy Spirit. When I speak of milk and meat, I am talking about the teachings of the scriptures.

Scripture Backup: *However, brothers and sisters, I could not talk to you as to spiritual people, but [**only**] as to worldly people [**dominated by human nature**], mere infants [**in the new lif**e] in Yahshua I fed you with milk, not solid food; for you were not yet able to receive it. Even now, you are still not ready. You are still worldly [**controlled by ordinary impulses, the sinful capacity**]. For as long as there is jealousy, strife, and discord among you, are you not unspiritual (**unfruitful**), and are you not walking like ordinary men [**unchanged by faith**]?*

Breakdown: One has to learn scripture and grow in a relationship with Yah through Yahshua to know his voice and follow His ways. As one walks in the ways of Yah through Yahshua and by being in a relationship with the Father. The fruits of the spirit will develop and mature to bear more fruit because one is anchored according to scripture, *every* good tree brings forth good fruit. Without fruit, no one can be filled. The unknown tongue is a gift that one receives, and gifts are given without repentance. I am

not saying that one does not fall short of Yah when being filled with the Holy Spirit but a person filled with the Holy Spirit will not want to willingly sin. The Holy Spirit will convict them to repent. However, when individuals come out of the world, they are not instantly filled with the fruits of the spirit (the **same as being filled with the Holy Spirit**).

The fruits of the spirit are the result of His presence within us which is love [**unselfishness-concern for others**], joy, [**inner**] peace, patience [**not the ability to wait, but how we act while waiting**], kindness, goodness, faithfulness, gentleness, self-control. Against such things, there is no law. And those who belong to Yahshua the Messiyah have **crucified the [1]sinful nature together with its passions and appetites**. As one is circumcised of the fleshly ways of their sinful nature, then the fruits of the spirits will manifest. They will be filled with the Holy Spirit. The fruits of the spirit will be evident in their character, and you will know them by their fruit. Again, some people who speak in an unknown tongue show no fruits of the spirit.

Matthew 7:16: By their fruit, you will recognize them [with **that is, by their contrived doctrine and self-focus**]. I have met people that speak in an unknown tongue that was mean as rattlesnakes, with no evidence of the fruits of the spirit at all. They have the gift of speaking in an unknown language but no fruit; I cannot stress enough that gifts come without repentance. Furthermore, it is dangerous to think that one is filled with the Holy Spirit because one speaks in an unknown tongue. Satan knows how to speak in tongues, and some churches call themselves teaching the unknown tongue. One cannot teach an unknown tongue that is sent from the third heaven.

Moreover, Apostle Shaul (Paul) expounds about an unknown tongue more than any other gift mentioned in 1 Corinthians in regards to building the body (**assembly**) of Yahshua. I suppose that the members of the Corinthian assembly were probably magnifying that particular gift just as it is today. Nevertheless, Apostle Shaul had to intervene. the sinful nature of many people wants to feel like they are better than other people by competing and comparing, so Apostle Shaul had to explain to them that the gift of an unknown tongue is actually for those that do not believe (**to help them believe**). It edifies the individual soul but does not edify the whole body to benefit from it. Therefore, Apostle Shaul expressed that he would rather speak five words of understanding to instruct others than ten thousand words in a tongue [**which others cannot understand**]. He emphasizes that if one desires to have the gift of tongues, to also asks for the gift of interpretation of the tongues so that the whole body can be edified by what is being said. Apostle Shaul stated that if I pray in an unknown tongue, my spirit prays, but my understanding is unfruitful. It is written in scripture that in everything to get understanding (**Proverbs 4:7**). *"The beginning of wisdom is to get [skillful and Yahly] wisdom [it is preeminent]!* ***And with all your acquiring, get understanding*** *[actively seek spiritual discernment, mature comprehension, and logical interpretation].*

A Pastor of a church I attended emphasized speaking in an unknown tongue and said, if you have not received the gift of speaking in tongues then there is sin in your life you are not doing. I know that my life had changed. The fruits of the spirits matched my character, especially love. I was walking upright before Yah and in a close relationship with Him, full of joy, and was using me to turn others to Him. Therefore, I was constantly examining myself, judging myself, seeking what could be wrong with my life and for what reason I had not received the gift of an unknown tongue. Therefore, when the Pastor made that statement, it made me feel condemned. When I should not have felt that way. However, Yah's mercy and grace brought me through. I remember it like it was yesterday. It was a call to the altar to get on your knees and pray to tarry for the unknown tongue as proof that you are filled with the Holy Spirit. I was on my knees and I heard His voice softly and lovingly. He said, "get up from there you are already filled with the Holy Spirit." I was so relieved but was a little puzzled because the church I attended taught hard that speaking in an unknown tongue is evident that you are filled with the Holy Spirit.

Yah is so kind and loving that he sent a man of Yah to my place of work at the time to break down what the gifts of speaking in an unknown tongue were all about from the book of **1 Corinthians**. Then I went home and turned on the radio. It was also confirmed through the teaching of Dr. Tony Evans. I was so full of joy and relieved all I could do was praise Yah, especially when I read, **"wherefore tongues are for a sign, not to them that believe, but to them that believe not. But prophesying serves, not for them that believe not, but for them which believe."** Therefore, when Yah told me that I am already filled and for me to get up from that altar asking for it I received it, and a weight lifted off of me. I know that the fruits of the spirit were evident in my character. I was also about two years into my walk as a believer. I was still early in learning the scriptures. Unfortunately, I attended a church that taught in error that the gift of tongues and being reborn of the Holy Spirit are the same, which are two separate things. The Pastor of the church that was teaching this lacked love; he had a spirit for the love of money and was full of pride and deception, but he spoke with the gift of an unknown tongue. **He that speaketh**

in an unknown tongue edifieth himself; but he that prophesieth edifieth the church. I would that ye all speak **with tongues but rather that ye prophesied:** for greater is he that **prophesieth than he that speaketh with tongues, except he interprets**, that the church may receive edifying. **So likewise, except you utter by the language words easy to be understood, how shall it be known what is spoken? For you shall speak into the air.**

Therefore, if I know not the meaning of the voice, I shall be unto him that speaketh a barbarian, and he that speaketh shall be a barbarian unto me (**not understanding each other's language**). Even so you, forasmuch are zealous of spiritual gifts, seek that ye may excel to the edifying of the church. Wherefore let him that speaketh in an unknown tongue pray that he may interpret. **For if I pray in an unknown tongue, my spirit prayeth, but my understanding is unfruitful.** What is it then? I will pray with the spirit, and I will pray with the understanding also: I will sing with the spirit, and I will sing with the understanding also. In the law, it is written, with men of other tongues and other lips will I speak to these people; yet they do not hear me, said Yah. **Wherefore tongues are for a sign, not to them that believe, but to them that believe not: But prophesying serve not for them that believe not, but for them which believe.** If therefore the whole church has come together into one place, and all speak with an unknown language, and those that are unlearned enters, or unbelievers, will they not say that you are mad? How is it then, brethren? When ye come together, every one of you has a psalm, have a doctrine, hath a tongue, have revelation, and have interpretation. Let all things be done unto edifying the body.

If any man speaks in an unknown tongue, let it be by two, or at the most by three, and let one interpret. **But if there be no interpreter, let him keep silence in the church; and let him speak to himself, and to Yah.**

John 15:26 I will send you a **helper**
John 16:13 Let the Holy Spirit lead you into all truth
John 14:12 You will do greater works
Galatians 5:22:23 the fruits of the Spirit [**the result of His presence within us**]
Romans 11:29: Giftings come without repentance
Matthew 3:8-10: So produce fruit that is consistent with repentance [**demonstrating new behavior that proves a change of heart and a conscious decision to turn away from sin**]
Matthew 7:16: By their fruit, you will recognize them [**that is, by their contrived doctrine and self-focus**].

Scriptures Proving To Be Filled and Reborn of the Holy Spirit

1 Thessalonians 4:7-8
that each of you knows how to control his own body in holiness and honor [**being available for Yah's purpose and separated from things profane**], not [**to be used**] in lustful passion, like the Gentiles who do not know Yah *and* are ignorant of His will.

Mark 16:16
He who has believed [**in Me**] and has been baptized will be saved [**from the penalty of Yah's wrath and judgment**], but he who has not believed will be condemned.

Romans 15:13
May the Yah of hope fill you with all joy and peace in

believing, so that by the power of the Holy Spirit you may abound in hope."

1 Corinthians 6:13
Do you not know that your bodies are temples of the Holy Spirit, who is in you, whom you have received from Yah? You are not your own.

Acts 1:8
But you will receive power when the Holy Spirit comes on you, and you will be my witnesses in Jerusalem

Isaiah 11:2
The Spirit of Yah will rest on him— the Spirit of wisdom and of understanding, the Spirit of counsel and of might, the Spirit of the knowledge and fear of Yah.

John 14:26
But the Advocate, the Holy Spirit, whom the Father will send in my name, will teach
you all things and will remind you of everything I have said to you.

Judges 3:10
The Spirit of Yah came on him so that he became Israel's judge and went to war.

Luke 24-45
Then he opened their minds so they could understand the Scriptures.

John 3:6-8
Flesh gives birth to flesh, but the Spirit gives birth to spirit. You should not be surprised at my saying, 'You must be

born again. The wind blows wherever it pleases. You hear
its sound, but you cannot tell where it comes from or where

it is going. **So it is with everyone born of the Spirit."**
(This last verse also is proof that everyone born of the
the spirit should discern the same things confirming
situations in one)

Micah 3:8
But as for me, I am filled with power, with the Spirit of
Yah, and with justice and might, to declare to Jacob his
transgression, to Israel his sin.

1 Corinthians 13
If I speak with the tongues of men and of angels but have
not [a]love [**for others growing out of Yah's love for me**],
then I have become only a noisy gong or a clanging cymbal
[**just an annoying distraction**]. [2] And if I have *the gift* of
prophecy [**and speak a new message from Yah to the**
people], and understand all mysteries, and [**possess**] all
knowledge; and if I have all [**sufficient**] faith so that I can
remove mountains, but do not have love [**reaching out to**
others], I am nothing. If I give all my possessions to
feed *the poor*, and if I surrender my body [b]to be burned,
but do not have love, it does me no good at all.

Chapter II
IS ONCE SAVED ALWAYS SAVED

Those of you that believe "ONCE SAVED ALWAYS
SAVED," Please read the following and see if it makes
sense to continue to believe that. According to the
following scriptures that is an error taught in churches for
years and it is important to repent from that belief so that
you can walk upright before the Most High.

IS ONCE SAVED ALWAYS SAVED?
What Does Saved Really Mean?

Webster's Dictionary Definition of "Saved"
1.) Keep safe or rescue from harm
2.) Keep and store up for future use

In this lesson, I will be coming from a biblical perspective of the word "saved." The word saved is only recorded 103 times in the 66 books. I say the 66 books "only" because some books have been removed from the bible. There are more than 66 books of the bible scriptures.

The Hebrew translation for saved is Mattenai (**4982**) meaning gift of Yahuah; generosity. Therefore, we know that Yahshua the son of Yah was given to the chosen people of Yah first and then the gentiles as a gift to atone for our sins. However, there is work to be done on each individual part after receiving Yahshua. That is to work out your own salvation by being a responsible follower of Yahshua through the word of Yah. This is not Tonida's opinion it is proven in the book of Philippians below. **Philippians 2:12**, says that everyone must work out their own soul salvation. Meaning that no one is responsible for your salvation but **YOU** when you become of age to understand. You chose either Yah's way or Satan's way. Therefore, **Philippians 2:12** is one of many scriptures to prove that it is more to being saved than quoting **Romans 10:9**, most leaders in your church teach that is all you have to do. However, you must make conscious decisions every day through self-evaluation and the choices you make by measuring yourself according to the word of Yah. Not comparing yourself to others but to the word of Yah; when you compare yourself to others, you become self-righteous because we all fall short of the word of Yah.

Philippians 2:12 says, so then, my dear ones, just as you have always obeyed [**my instructions with enthusiasm**], not only in my presence but now much more in my absence, continue to work out your salvation [**that is, cultivate it, bring it to full effect, actively pursue spiritual maturity**] with awe-inspired fear and trembling [**using serious caution and critical self-evaluation to avoid anything that might offend Yah or discredit the name of Yahshua**]."
Greek translation and definition of saved (**4982**) – to save, rescue, deliver, to heal; by extension: to be in right relationship with Yah; with the implication that the condition before salvation was one of grave danger and distress; saved, made whole, healed, do well, preserve.
Now let us look at what salvation means. The Hebrew translation (**4991**) means gift or something given.

Salvation: Recorded 165 times in the 66 books of the Bible Greek Translation of Salvation (**4991**): Rescue, deliverance, the state of not being in grave danger and being safe; this can refer to ordinary dangers and conditions on earth but it usually refers to believers being safe from Yah's wrath by being in a proper relationship with Yah.

Hebrew 3:12-14 my friends watch out! Do not let evil thoughts or doubts make any of you turn from the living Yah. You must encourage one another each day. Moreover, you must keep going while there is still a time that can be called "today." If you do not, then sin may fool some of you and make you stubborn. We were sure about Yahshua when we first became his people. So let us hold tightly to our faith until the end.

First verses (12) - for our weapons of warfare are not carnal but mighty through Yahshua and casting down imaginations (**thoughts that enter the mind that is unyahly**) under the submission of the word of Yah

The second verse (13) – Admonish one another (**point out each other's errors in love**) to keep from falling and avoid judgment. Seek Yah while He may be found; call on Him [for salvation] while He is near (**Isaiah 55:6**). verse (13)

While you have the Light, believe and trust in the Light [have faith in it, hold on to it, rely on it], so that you may become sons of Light [being filled with Light as followers of Yahshua]." **John 12:36** verse (13)

But Yahshua said to him, "No one who puts his hand to the plow and looks back [to the things left behind] is fit for the kingdom of Yah." verse (13)
Mark 1:16
and saying, "The [**appointed period of**] time is fulfilled, and the kingdom of Yah is at hand; repent [**change your inner self—your old way of thinking, regret past sins, live your life in a way that proves repentance; seek Yah's purpose for your life**] and believe [**with a deep, abiding trust**] the good news [**regarding salvation**]."
Hebrews 10:36-39
Keep on being brave! It will bring you great rewards. Learn to be patient, so you will please Yah and be given what he has promised. As Scripture says, "Yahshua is coming soon! It will not be very long. The people Yah accepts will live because of their faith. But he isn't pleased with anyone who turns back." We are not like those people who turn back and are destroyed. We will keep on having faith until we are saved.

Commentary: Really I can stop right here at the scripture above (**Hebrews 10:36-39**) to wrap this up. However, there are more scriptures I need you to understand and point out that "once saved always saved" is a lie taught in churches for years which will get those who believe that lie tossed into the lake of fire on judgment day if they do not repent. Believing in that lie is the reason why many Christians feel like they can consciously commit all kinds of sins and think that Yah is ok with it. Taking for granted that Yahshua died nailed to the stake for the sins of people that come to Yah through His son Yahshua, and treat Yah's grace and the death of Yahshua in vain. Many Christians always bring up the scripture "we are saved by His grace" found in the book of **Ephesians 2:8**. That is very true, nevertheless, there is still work to be done on your part by having a relationship with Yah through His son Yahshua so that your name will not be blotted out of the book of life (**Revelations 3:5**).

He that overcometh, the same shall be clothed in white raiment, and I will not blot out his name out of the book of life, but I will confess his name before my Father, and before his angels.

Now tell me how could it be possible to still live a sinful life and live eternal with Yah, if it is possible that your name can be blotted out of the book of life? Pay attention to what is underlined "HE WHO OVER COMETH."

To "overcome" falls under the category of, afflictions, hardships, trials, tribulations, long-sufferings, endurance, persecutions, failers, lack of faith, temptations, etc. Because each day has its troubles (**Matthew 6:34**) and we have to depend on the word of Yah and be submissive to the Holy Spirit to guide us into all truth (**John 16:13**). This comes from examining ourselves daily to make sure that we are aligning our lives with the righteousness of Yahshua as He was an example to us by following the word of Yah and having a relationship with Yah.

Romans 6:23 For the wages of sin is death, but the gift of Yah [that is, His remarkable, overwhelming gift of grace to believers] is eternal life in Yahshua our Adonai.

John 8:47
He that is of Yah heareth Yah's words: ye, therefore, hear
them not, because ye are not of Yah.
Those that are of Yah, hear His voice, if he/she does not hear
His voice he belongs to him NOT.

John 10:26-29
But ye believe not, because ye are not of my sheep, as I said
unto you. My sheep hear my voice, and I know them, and they
follow me: And I give unto them eternal life, and they shall
never perish; neither shall any man pluck them out of my
hand. My Father, which gave him me, is greater than all; and
no man can pluck them out of my Father's hand.

Many Christians I have spoken to like to use the scripture
that says no one can pluck you out of Yah's hands.
Nevertheless, they are not reading the verses above that
scripture. Starting with verse 26. However, if anyone turns
from the truth they will no longer follow the voice of Yah
through Yahshua. Again, John 10:27 says, "My sheep hear
my voice, and I know them, and they will follow me. If you
are hearing the voice of Yah, you will not want to sin at
will because that inner voice of Yah will convict you from
doing so.
The Greek dictionary of the New Testament says that the
meaning of pluck for that scripture means: "pluck or pull
by force." Therefore, no one can take you from the hand of
Yah. However, one can jump out of the His hand if they
decide to give up their salvation by simply denying Yah's
truth and turning to false doctrines of demons. Remember
the breakdown of salvation. Let me reiterate scripture **1
Timothy 4:1** But the [Holy] Spirit openly and
unmistakably declares that in later times some will turn

away from the faith, paying attention to deceitful and seductive spirits and doctrines of demons. 1 **Timothy 5:15** for some have already turned aside after Satan.

There is a misunderstanding of **Romans 10:9** that if thou shalt confess with your mouth Yahshua is ruler, and shalt believe in your heart that Yah has raised him from the dead, you shalt be saved. There is more to this scripture, even Satan and demons believe **Romans 10:9**, and witnessed it too, nevertheless, they are not trying to repent and do what is right. Please go back and read the verses before verse nine. Verse 2-4

2 For I bear them record that they have a zeal of Yah not according to knowledge.

3 For them being ignorant of Yah's righteousness, and going about to establish their own righteousness, have not submitted themselves unto the righteousness of Yah.

4 For Yahshua is the end of the law for righteousness to everyone that believeth.

Romans 8:2-9

There is therefore now no condemnation to them, which are in Christ Jesus, who walk not after the flesh, but after the Spirit. For the law of the Spirit of life in Yahshua, the Messiah hath made me free from the law of sin and death. For what the law could not do, in that it was weak through the flesh, Yah sending his own Son in the likeness of sinful flesh, and for sin, condemned sin in the flesh: That the righteousness of the law might be fulfilled in us, who walk after the flesh does mind the things of the flesh, but they that are after the Spirit the things of the Spirit. For to be carnally minded is death, but to be spiritually minded is life and peace. Because the carnal mind is enmity against Yah: for it is not subject to the law of Yah, neither indeed can be.

they that are in the flesh cannot please Yah. But ye are not in the flesh, but in the Spirit, if so be that the Spirit of Yah dwells in you. Now if any man has not the Spirit of Yahshua, he is none of his. And if Yahshua is in you, the body is dead because of sin; but the Spirit is life because of righteousness.

But if the Spirit of him that raised up Yahshua from the dead dwell in you, he that raised up Yahshua from the dead shall also quicken your mortal bodies by his Spirit that dwelleth in you. Therefore, brethren, we are debtors, not to the flesh, to live after the flesh. For if ye live after the flesh, ye shall die: but if ye through the Spirit do mortify the deeds of the body, ye shall live. For as many as are led by the Spirit of Yah, they are the sons of Yah.

There are many other scriptures too but I cut it short so that I will not have a Minnie book posted. I advise you to research your scriptures further and study the scriptures found in this post and decide if you still believe "Once Saved Is Always saved.

CHAPTER III

DANGERS OF USING PROFANITY
AS A BELIEVER

Proverbs 18:21
Death and life are in the power of the tongue,
And those who love it *and* indulge in it will eat its
fruit *and* bear the consequences of their words.

Ephesians 4:29 [29] Do not let unwholesome [**foul, profane, worthless, vulgar**] words ever come out of your mouth, but only such *speech* as is good for building up others, according to the need *and* the occasion, so that it will be a blessing to those who hear [**you speak**].

Ephesians 5:4 [4] Let there be no filthiness and silly talk, or coarse [**obscene or vulgar**] joking *because* such things are not appropriate [**for believers**]; but instead, speak of your thankfulness [**to Yah**]. **An example is,** men and women, talking to their friends about their x using obscene and vulgar words and language. **Colossians 3:8** Now rid yourselves [**completely**] of all these things: anger, rage, malice, slander, and obscene (**abusive, filthy, vulgar**) language from your mouth.

Matthew 12:36 [36] But I tell you, on the day of judgment people will have to give an account for every careless *or* useless word they speak. [37] For by your words [**reflecting your spiritual condition**] you will be justified *and* acquitted of the guilt of sin, and by your words [**rejecting Me**] you will be condemned *and* sentenced." Yes, everyone will have to give an account for every useless word used so be mindful of what you say.

James 1:26 If anyone thinks himself to be religious [**scrupulously observant of the rituals of his faith**], and does not control his tongue but deludes his *own* heart, this person's religion is worthless (**futile, barren**).

James 3:6 And the tongue is [**in a sense**] a fire, the *very* world of injustice *and* unrighteousness; the tongue is set among our members as that which contaminates the entire body, and sets on fire the course of our life [**the cycle of man's existence**], and in itself set on fire by [b]hell (**Gehenna**).

James 3:8-10

But no one can tame the *human* tongue; it is a restless evil [**undisciplined, unstable**], full of deadly poison. [9] With it we bless our Father Yah, and with it we curse men, who have been made in the likeness of Yah. [10] Out of the same mouth come to *both* blessings and cursing. These things, my brothers, should not be this way [**for we have a moral obligation to speak in a manner that reflects our fear of Yah and profound respect for His precepts**].

2 Timothy 2:16 But avoid all irreverent babble and yahless chatter [**with its profane, empty words**], for it will lead to further unyahliness, [17] and their teaching will spread like gangrene.

Psalm 34:13-14 Keep your tongue from evil and your lips from speaking lies. [14] Turn away from evil and do good; Seek peace and pursue it.

Proverbs 15:1;4

A soft *and* gentle *and* thoughtful answer turns away wrath, but harsh *and* painful *and* careless words stir up anger.
A soothing tongue [**speaking words that build up and encourage**] is a tree of life,
But a perversive tongue [**speaking words that overwhelm and depress**] crushes the spirit.

Proverbs 4:24 Put away from you a deceitful (**lying, misleading**) mouth,
And put devious lips far from you.

PRAYER OF REPENTANCE

Father Yah, learning your laws regarding foul language. I come to you with a heart of repentance and I ask that you forgive me. I ask for your mercy and grace. I invite the Holy Spirit in my heart to lead and guide me. To sustain my tongue when I get the urge to cuss. To bring to my mind a word to replace the passion I am feeling at that time when I need to express how I am feeling. Help me to remember your law that says, " to be angry but not sin." I ask that you deliver me from this spirit. I am believing you to help me with my strong tongue. I realize it cannot be done in my own strength but I need your help. Deliver me from all insecurities, past hurts that scared me deeply, and abuse that aided this anxiety to cause a cussing spirit to enter me. According to your laws, I am asking you to help me to guard my tongue and cover my mouth. Keep watch over the door of my lips to keep me from speaking thoughtlessly. In Yahshua's name, I pray. Halleluyah.

SCRIPTURES FOR REPENTANCE OF THE FOUL MOUTH

Psalms 141:3 Set a guard, O Yah, cover my mouth; Keep watch over the door of my lips **[to keep me from speaking thoughtlessly]**.

Proverbs 21:23 He who guards his mouth and his tongue, guards himself against troubles.

Luke 6:45 The [**intrinsically**] good man produces what is good *and* honorable *and* moral out of the good

treasure [**stored**] in his heart; and
the [**intrinsically**] evil *man* produces what is
wicked *and* depraved out of the evil [**in his heart**]; for his
mouth speaks from the overflow of his heart.

The scripture "to be angry but not sin," mean not to miss
the mark, and ask Yah to help you with the anxiety you are
feeling. His law says, be not anxious for nothing.

Ephesians 4:26: BE ANGRY [**at sin—at immorality, at
injustice, at ungodly behavior**], YET DO NOT SIN; do not let
your anger [**cause you shame, nor allow it to**] last until the
sun goes down.

Jeremiah 17:17
"Blessed [**with spiritual security**] is the man who
believes *and* trusts in *and* relies on Yah
And whose hope *and* confident expectation are in Yah.

CHAPTER IV

JUDGING OF OTHERS

**What Does It Mean Biblically To Judge Someone
Matthew 7:1-6**

Judging Others
Do not judge *and* criticize *and* condemn [**others unfairly
with an attitude of self-righteous superiority as though
assuming the office of a judge**] so that you will not be
judged [**unfairly**]. [2] For just as you [**hypocritically**] judge
others [**when you are sinful and unrepentant**], so will
you be judged; and by your standard of measure [**used to
pass out judgment**], judgment will be measured to
you. [3] Why do you look at the [**insignificant**] speck that is
in your brother's eye, but do not notice *and* acknowledge
the [**egregious**] log that is in your own eye? [4] Or how can
you say to your brother, 'Let me get the speck out of your
eye,' when there is a log in your own eye? [5] You hypocrite
(**play-actor, pretender**), first get the log out of your own
eye, and then you will see clearly to take the speck out of
your brother's eye."Do not give that which is holy
to [b]dogs, and do not throw your pearls before pigs, for they
will trample them under their feet, and turn and tear you to
pieces (**meaning that they are carnally minded and
cannot understand the things of the spirit and will
attack you for it**).

WE ARE TO ADMONISH ONE ANOTHER
Colossians 3:16-17
Let the [**spoken**] word of Christ have its home within you
[**dwelling in your heart and mind—permeating every aspect
of your being**] as you teach [**spiritual things**] and
admonish *and* train one another with all wisdom, singing psalms
and hymns and spiritual songs with thankfulness in your hearts

to Yah. Whatever you do [**no matter what it is**] in word or deed, do everything in the name of the Yahshua [**and in dependence on Yah**], giving thanks to Yah the Father through Him.

For example:

1. If you are fornicating (**having sex and not married**), you cannot judge someone for committing adultery (**which is having sex with a married individual**). You are no better.
2. If you are stealing from your job by taking paper, pencils, ink pens, toilet paper, bottled water, etc. You cannot judge the person that steals something from a store because you are just as guilty as they are. Stealing is stealing.

3. If you are coveting (**meaning desiring something someone else has**) your neighbor's house or car you cannot judge someone for coveting another man or woman's spouse.

AgainMatthew 7:1-6

Do not judge *and* criticize *and* condemn [**others unfairly with an attitude of self-righteous superiority as though assuming the office of a judge**], so that you will not be judged [**unfairly**]. ² For just as you [**hypocritically**] judge others [**when you are sinful and unrepentant**], so will you be judged; and by your standard of measure [**used to pass out judgment**], judgment will be measured to you.

CHAPTER V

YAH IS A JEALOUS YAH
AND HAS A RIGHT TO BE

Shalom everyone and welcome back to "Warriors for Yah. This is a quick message to give Yah the glory that is due to Him. All videos I make will most likely refer back to scriptures, even my poems. Therefore, the scriptures will be placed in the description box for you to read for yourselves.

Starting with…..Exodus 34:13
But you shall tear down *and* destroy their [**pagan**] altars, smash in pieces their [**sacred**] pillars (**obelisks, images**) and cut down their [b]Asherim 14 —for you shall not worship any other god; for Yah, whose name is Jealous, is a jealous (**impassioned**) Yah [**demanding what is rightfully and uniquely His**] Yah is responsible for many miracles but does not get the honor that is due to Him for doing so. I am sure we can all think of things in our lives that were a close call, but because of Yah's grace and mercy, they passed us by. I know I have many of them, and quite a few are near-death experiences. Satan tried to kill me from birth you'll, I will be talking more about that in another video soon so stay tuned.

For example, People that are not giving Yah the honor and glory that belongs to Him. However, they may be grateful for their lives being spared or saved from a tragic thing happening to them, but they will say things like. I thank my lucky stars, or I thank the universe, I thank my ancestors (**most of the time talking about dead ancestors at that**), and last but not least, I would hear, whoooo, that was a close one. Nevertheless, always give Yah the glory for it. **Now I know I am about to stomp on some toes but the truth has to be told. Dead ancestors are not keeping you from trouble or directing you in any kind of way.**

According to **Ecclesiastes 9:4-6**
For the living know that they will die; but the dead know nothing, and they no longer have a reward [**of service for what they did here on earth**], for the memory of them is forgotten. **6** Indeed their love, their hatred, and their zeal have already perished (**meaning their soul is no longer active in the land of the living**), and they will no longer have a share [**in this age**] in anything that is done under the sun.

For the first verse, I know some will say, well that is not true because my Mother, Father, and/or child, etc. passed away but I think about them all the time. When I first heard this, I was thinking the same thing many of you are thinking. However, I thought about my grandmother, and as much as I loved my grandmother, she passed away when I was fifteen. I'm now in my 50's so we know that was some time ago. When she first passed, I thought about her every day intensely (**her memories and character**) for 5 years. However, as the years went on. She would pop up in my mind occasionally, or if I look at my photo albums or a family member that reminded me of a character trait she had. For the most part, as much as I loved her, she will always be with me in my memory. However, I do not think of her as much now as I used to but I will never forget her.

The second verse is stating the point that dead people's character and souls no longer are with us, and they no longer can share in this age of the living with anything that is done under the sun. When I was researching and reading scriptures, I could not help for thinking about when the Israelites were led into the wilderness to get to the promised land and how Yah saved them from being killed by the pharaoh and his army. Yah fed them with food falling from the sky and gave Moses instructions to strike the rock so that water can come from it to drink. Yet, they were still complaining and not giving Yah the glory for what he has done or they soon forgot. I said to Yah. I get upset when people are not appreciative when I do things for them. However, you are Yah and it should never happen to you, but it does so I need not complain and remember to give you praise in all things.

When Moses went to the mountaintop to speak with Yah for 40 days and forty nights with no food and water (**Exodus 34:28**), the children of Israel that were waiting for Moses to come back ended up melting down their gold and making an idol image of a bull or cow to worship. Giving the idol figure the praises that belong to Yah from what they were saved from. Just as it happened then, it is the same today. Many people give everything and everybody else the praise and glory for their blessings but Yah.

Sometimes when I hear stories of people near death experiences or the danger they escaped. I give Yah the praises, even if they do not. If they are giving Him praise, I am praising Him right along with them if they know me or not. If they do not give Yah the glory, I will, because I know that it was nobody but the mercy and grace of Yah that spared them from that tragedy or demise. Let everything that has breath praise Yah (**Psalms 150:6**).

When the birds chirp they praise Yah. When dogs bark
they praise Yah when a cat meow it is praising Yah when a
rooster crows Yah is being praised. Therefore every human
being with breath should praise Yah. We were created to
worship Yah, and give Him praise.
Halleluyah!!!!....Remember Halleluyah means praise you
Yah.

1) Start your day with Yah, by giving thanks for
another day to have a chance at serving Him, by
using your mouth to talk about the goodness He has
done in your life. That is giving Him recognition
and praise.

2.) Make a list of the things you are thankful for

3.) Take note of things that we take for granted. Thank
Yah for the beautiful pastures of grass, the breeze
blowing in the air, and the sun that overtakes the
clouds. Imagine if we did not have the sun; the
grayish atmosphere that would bring depression.
Yah not only made the sun to give us heat and for
gardening but for our reception of life, he knows
that sunshine helps to bring happiness to mankind.
Be thankful to Yah that you have all of your limbs
and body functions. Be grateful that you have not
lost your mind because of the unpleasant encounters
of life but you are in the right mind. Be thankful to
Yah that your situation is not worse than it could be.
Have you ever heard the saying, "there was a man
that complained he had no shoes and looked to his
right and saw a man with no feet?
Always know there is someone that is doing worse
than you. Give Yah thanks in all things he is
worthy. No matter your circumstance, He always
makes a way.

4.) Last but not least, learn to Love yourself and be concerned for others; I saved this for last because many of us do not love ourselves enough. Has always put others first and neglected ourselves, most of the time it stems from something having to do with upbringing but that is another lesson in itself. I know because I used to be that way. People love your selflessness about you, but the world is filled with people that are always in need, and if you do not take the time to love yourself and take care of yourself.

Your life will pass you by, and you will be drained and look old for your age because you always looking out for others without no one looking out for you and it will suck the life out of you and make you drained. Yah's command is to love one another, help one another, confess your sins to one another, and pray for one another. He did not say, to be one-sided and for one to do all the work in a relationship to make it healthy, but for both to give in to the relationship. Not to leave the other hanging. People can be selfish, they will get what they need out of you and keep going, and that is under many categories. My people lack this command of Yah and it is a part of the curses spoken over us as a nation because of the sin against Yah. Those of you who know we are the true chosen people of Yah know what I am talking about.

Moreover, love others. This is the opposite of learning to love yourself. Many people in this world are self-centered and conceited. They want to be the center of attention and think that their needs and wants are always the most important before anything or anyone at all times. This issue also generally stems from an unbalanced upbringing. You see how everything still boils down to needing Yah and following the instructions of His law, how we are to live and treat one another? He knows the end from the beginning and knows that humans would act this way. The rules of the government were originally put in place according to the scriptures believe it or not. However, as sin increases, the world is sinking more and more into wickedness with the laws that are in place, which is in opposition to putting laws in place that are in violation of the laws of Yah. Perilous times are here on earth already and will get worse, and Yah's judgment upon the earth will increase as well.

According to Matthew 24:12, because wickedness shall abound, the love of many shall wax cold. **Furthermore, Matthew 12 6-11** is Yahshua talking to his disciples and he says, "for many shall come in my name, saying, I am the Messiyah; and shall deceive many.[6] And ye shall hear of wars and rumors of wars: see that ye be not troubled: for all these things must come to pass, but the end is not yet. [7] For nation shall rise against nation, and kingdom against kingdom: and there shall be famines, and pestilences, and earthquakes, in many ' places (**that never were**).[8] All these are the beginning of sorrows.[9] Then shall they deliver you up to be afflicted, and shall kill you: and ye shall be hated of all nations for my name's sake.[10] And then shall many be offended, and shall betray one another, and shall hate one another.[11] And many false prophets shall rise, and shall deceive many. The bottom line is to give honor to Yah where credit is due. Never forget what Yah has done and still doing and give Him praise for it.

CHAPTER VI

YOUR HUSBAND IS YOUR MAKER

I was led to give this message to my sisters because there is a demonic attack on the sisters. Women were always blamed for everything as if we are the only ones involved with whatever topic became an issue. Starting with Eve. Yah has given me a revelation about that too which I included in this book. Another example from the bible is regarding the woman caught in adultery by the Pharisees and scribes brought to Yahshua to stone, but they did not bring the man, and he was just as guilty as she was. However, Yahshua is so fair, He told the disciples to cast the first stone if any of them were not guilty of sin and each one left starting with the eldest to the youngest. The story of Bathsheba has been miss-taught; she was not on the roof bathing. David was on his roof walking and looked down at her. Nevertheless, Bathsheba gets the bad rap as if she was trying to entice with her body and she did not have a clue that David was watching her.

This teaching is not about man bashing, but this is to encourage sisters to put all their trust in Yah and be more concerned about pleasing Him in this day and time. Many of our men are out of order, not all but many. As far as being the head, many do not have the discipline, and compassion, are humble before Yah to guide them on how to be a husband, and lack accountability to be good husbands and fathers. Many of them complain that it is hard to find a sister without children but their absents make up the ratio by not marrying the woman or any of the women they have gotten pregnant with. They are at fault for sowing their seeds all over the place with no commitment. Therefore, no one can point the finger at the other, because there is blame to be had on both parties. The sister and the brother are wrong for committing fornication, which leads to a child out of wedlock where there is no commitment on the behalf of the absent parent. Yes, because the sister did not make wise choices as many of us have not. Just keeping it real. She will bear more responsibility because the absent parent is not in the household as a husband to take on full responsibility. However, they were both in error in the first place for fornicating. The brother is just as guilty knowing that he had no intentions, or thinking about making the sister their wife but lays with her and gets her or many other women pregnant with no kind of commitment.

I am here to encourage you sisters to find your truth and what your call is while seeking a healthy relationship with Yah. Your joy in the Father, who is also your husband according to His law, will take care of you like a husband. I am not saying I was an angel or ever was. I am telling you this because of all my faults and messed up life at one time. Did not know if I was coming or going, but I am living proof of what I am saying. That is why I have the authority to speak about this. My sisters if you leave it up to society and brute beast men, men that are in darkness that put the daughters of Yah down with degrading words. You will hate yourself. Yah's sons or daughters have no room to put each other down. Both are in error with issues against the word of Yah. Because we are in the last days and Yah is moving quickly. I advise you to get closer to

Yah as much as you can. If He sees fit for you to have a physical husband; He will send you a husband with a heart of his own. However, you have to be right too, by spending time with Yah. He will change you and prepare you to be the virtuous woman you need to be. Now some sisters did not think that it was important for the man she is dating to have a good foundation with Yah leading him in his walk. The only thing she needed to know is that he goes to church and can quote scriptures. There is a big difference between a man just going to church and quoting scriptures, and a man letting Yah lead him, as a man of Yah should be. Because guess what? Satan goes to church and quotes scriptures too, but he does not submit to Yah as his head and follow his lead.

Therefore, it is not enough for your earthly husband my sisters to quote scriptures and go to church. He needs to be submissive to Yah with a contrite heart while being in a relationship trusting his word to know how to be an effective husband to you.

Now on the other hand sisters, you must also meet those same values to be a fit wife for a Yahly man. You must be a virtuous woman as scripture speaks about found in **Proverbs 31:10-31**. I do not want to get away from the topic but I needed to lay that down before I go any further with this lesson.

I will now give my testimony as to how Yah was not only a Father to me but a husband too. My sisters, many of you, are as if I once was. I wanted to get married so badly. I could taste it. During that time, I felt that way. I was a a single mother and I was a good mother but I wanted a husband that walks with Yah as his headship, to help me raise my child. A husband that could lead our family to be equally yoked as scripture speaks. I am going to use my own experience as evidence that Yah will be your Husband and help a single mother to raise her child/children. I am a virtuous woman, and I was during the time I wanted to get married so badly. I worked hard, cooked, cleaned, loved doing things as a family, very loving person, and believed in catering to my husband if I had one. In fact, if I had a husband, all I ever wanted to do was help my husband with whatever he was called to do and raise our children. However, Yah called me to do more than that. He consecrated me before I was placed in my mother's womb and set aside to be used. All the things I have been through in life I should have lost my mind. However, Yah kept me, and I had to go through all of that according to my call and His purpose for my life.

When I first came to Yah about wanting a husband, he told me to list the reasons why I wanted a husband. As I named the reasons, I realized he was already meeting those needs because of my relationship with Him. He helped me to raise my daughter too. The only thing that was not being met was the physical part. However, he did keep me. I fell short years in between when I was lonely and let my flesh get in the way, and broke my celibacy (**5-7 years in between**). However, I found out later why that happened and I will go into that in a later video, as the Holy Spirit leads.

    1.) Raised my daughter on temporary agencies. Had no benefits, but I never got sick, the lights were never out, and we always had food and decent clothing. I also had a mortgage for a very nice home. However, I lost the home after 5 years. I will go into detail regarding that, in another message, from another video. I had to pay for daycare, trips with the school, Mortgage, utilities, phone, food, be a good role model as a woman, denied myself of many things, sacrifice, encouraged my child when she was down, mentoring, exercised self-control, discipline, walk in faith by practicing what I preach and other responsibilities, all by the grace and help of Yah. He helped me to get through it and to do it.

2.) My daughter was so well-behaved and respectful people thought I had a husband because she was so well-balanced. My income was nowhere near, what I make today, and when I look back, being a single parent with very little income but all the responsibility, and Yah being in my life balanced things out. It was very hard, but much of the growth in Yah came from that period of my life. I believed him for fixing things in the house because I could not afford it, and Yah did it. For example, a pipe in the kitchen was leaking but I could not afford a plumber so I asked Yah to supernaturally fix it and He did. I tell you no lie.

3.) When I was trying to get out of a relative's house with my daughter because it was not safe. I could not afford the price of rent on my own, which was decent. Therefore, I signed up for Housing assistance and when I did, there was a two-year waiting list. However, with prayer and trusting

Yah, I received an offer within two months. I was never one to sleep late nor was my daughter. However, when we moved into our new place. Yah allowed us to sleep so peacefully. I awakened at 12:05 pm and my daughter awakened at 12:10 pm. It was so nice to be in our own place of safety.

4.) I liked getting my nails done just like the next sister. However, I could not afford it. Therefore, I saved money to get my nails done and looked at what the shop used and went to Rite Aid to buy the equipment, and started doing my own nails and making my own designs. I could not afford to go to the hairdresser, as I wanted to, therefore. I learned to do my own hair or I would wear wigs (**until Yah told me to stop**).

5.) My daughter did very well in school and she mined me with the utmost respect. My point is, Yah did this for me, and he will surely do it for you. I will make another video as a part 2 with more examples of how you can trust Yah to be what you need Him to be and do. The following are scriptures Regarding women of the bible, I was speaking about. I encourage you to read them.
I remember one day leaving my keys in the door all night long with no screen door, and I lived in the projects but no one came into my apartment.

6.) Another time, I did not close the door tightly and thought it was shut and locked. It was very windy

7.) that night but Yah had angels watching over my daughter and me because in the morning when I got up to wash clothes. The door blew open just as nicely. Yah is a keeper and a protector. I know that my listeners are thinking, "She really cares less about locking her door." However, I was very responsible and made sure of those things. However, I believe Yah allowed me to do it purposely to show me that He is a protector, and He got the glory out of it. Because each time that happened, I was so grateful and could not stop praising Him. I am still giving Him the glory for it and telling you about it as a testimony.

My Sisters There Are Three Major Things You Need To Do for Yah to Watch Over Yourself and Your Children Too

1.) Seek The Kingdom of Yah (**Matthew 6:33-34**) His word says to, "first and most importantly seek (**aim at, strive after**) His kingdom and His righteousness [**His way of doing and being right— the attitude and character of Yah**], and all these things will be given to you also. "You need not worry about tomorrow; for tomorrow will worry about itself. Each day has enough trouble of its own.

2.) Draw unto Yah & He will draw unto you (**James 4:8**) Come close to Yah [**with a contrite heart**] and He will come close to you. Wash your hands, from sin; and purify your hearts

3.) Bring your Burdens to Him (**Psalm 55:22**) Cast your burden on Yah [**release it**] and He will sustain *and* uphold you; He will never allow the righteous to be shaken (slip, fall, fail). As long as you keep your eyes on Him. Sometimes, we take

our eyes off Yah and start to slip, fall, and fail.
Repent turning from your wicked ways
(Chronicles 7:14) Yah says, "My people, who are
called by My Name, humble themselves, and pray
and seek (meaning **crave, as a necessity**), seek my
face and turn from their wicked ways (which are
unyahly ways), then I will hear [**them**] from
heaven, and forgive their sin and heal their land.

My sisters Stop fornicating, Stop Masturbating: I
know that many think that there is nothing wrong
with masturbating because there is nothing written
in the bible that says so. However, Yah gave me a
revelation during the time I was struggling with this
issue. I am being real my sisters because I am
trying to help you depend on Yah for any and
everything that seems impossible in the natural. If
your heart truly desires to stop sinning from
something, you are struggling with. He will deliver
you from it. I had no husband so when the urge
came I took care of it. However, when I told Yah I
need for Him to be my Husband and do deliver me
from that until He sends me a husband if it is His
will, He did it. Because each time, I did it, I felt bad
about it and I kept going to Yah about it. He
delivered me from it.

The revelation that Yah gave me is that, since you have
no husband to take care of your physical needs, you are
imagining a random man that is not your husband that
is pleasing you to the wild imagination. Therefore, you
are still committing fornication and sinning against

your own body. This also opens doors for demons to join in this self-gratification.

My Sisters Stop showing cleavage and other parts of the body there is nothing attractive about it. It might be sexy but not attractive for a virtuous-seeking woman through Yah. When I say sexy, I do not mean attractive as if the world means it. I am saying exactly what it says, "SEXY" means drawing men to you sexually. Showing body parts draw men with lust demons hovering over them and want to sex your sexy self up, with nothing but sex being involved to deposit his sperm, and then he is out. I know that the world wants to say it is another word for attractive but in the spiritual realm it means being drawn to sex. Especially when they dressed provocatively. We as women of Yah are to dress modestly which includes covering up.

When you get a chance, please read the scriptures regarding the:

Virtuous Woman- Proverbs 31:10-31

Woman caught in Adultery- John 8:1-11

When King David Peeked Bathsheba 2 Samuel 11:2-5

I say when King David peaked in on Bathsheba because he was on the roof of his palace looking down where he can see the living quarters of individuals from his roof by looking down.

Hope this was an encouraging message to my sisters that are single parents that do not know how they are going to make it. All I can say from experience is to trust Yah. I love you but Yah loves you best.

CHAPTER VII

Yah Is Fine With One Being Single
&
Soley Focus on the Kingdom of Yah

Matthew 19: 10-12
[**His**] disciples said to him, "If that is the case of a man with his wife, it is better not to marry." He answered, "Not all can accept [**this**] word, but only those to whom that is granted. Some are incapable of marriage because they were born so; some, because they were made so by others; some, because they have renounced marriage for the sake of the kingdom of heaven. Whoever can accept this ought to accept it."

For those who do not desire to get married because they are sold out for Yah. I believe Yah removes the desire to burn in lust physically to get married to quench that burn. It is normal for the hormones to react that way which is part of the attraction of a husband and wife for lovemaking. Paul said it is better to marry than to burn (**1 Corinthians 7:8-9**). **Apostle Paul continues:** Now to the unmarried and to widows, I say: it is a good thing for them to remain as they are, as I do, but if they cannot exercise self-control they should marry, for it is better to marry than to be on fire. [10] To the married, however, I give this instruction (**not I, but Yahshua**):
A wife should not separate from her husband—and if she does separate she either must remain single or become reconciled to her husband—and a husband should not divorce his wife.
Personally, for me, **Matthew 19:10-12** convinced me this is a fact not only from my own experience but also because of how Yah uses some people. There are so many demands on the life of some servants of Yah, and their life for the kingdom that there is really no time for marriage. Yah

respects marriage and expects each spouse to meet the other's needs. However, Yah and His kingdom still come first.

For those that falsely perceive the wrong thing in my message by thinking I am advocating not to get married. That is not what I am saying. Yah honors marriage and wants people to marry and be fruitful. Nevertheless, at the same time, in these last days of perilous times, there is a lot of work to do and Yah is demanding many of His servants to work like soldiers and warriors for the KINDOM. To whom much is given, much is required. Unless both are on fire and willing to put in the work with iron sharpening iron. We are in a spiritual battle constantly and many people that proclaim to be followers of Yah are spiritually lazy, including spouses.

Even Apostle Paul made the statement he would for individuals to be like him and choose not to get married and work for the Kingdom because he was more concerned about the Kingdom than Yah. By all means, marriage is a beautiful thing when both are equally yoked but there is a lot of work in a marriage, and Satan and his demons attack marriages because it is sacred. I do not advocate being shacked up either. As Paul said, if you burning to be physical, then you should get married. However, I will not stop at what Paul said; I will go on to say. Not to get married only to satisfy a physical urge but to pray for Yah to deliver you from those desires while you are single. He will do it, ask me how I know.

CHAPTER VIII

STOP PUTTING ALL THE BLAME ON EVE

The title of this lesson derived from a deep feeling of frustration every time somebody blames "Eve" for the fall of humankind but after receiving a "revelation" from Yah about this, I had to share it. Now do not get me wrong if she is truly responsible for all the blame then so be it. The truth is that she is not the full blame, she just happened to bite the fruit first. I hate to hear people make the comment, **"if it was not for Eve."** You will soon find out what I mean in a moment but I want to lay down the foundation first. I want you all to know that I did not feel this way in the beginning when I first read about Eve being the reason for the start of man's downfall. What made me want to go to Yah regarding this subject even more so is when the men speak on this subject as it gives them the satisfaction of being able to blame the woman. I started wondering if Adam was in another part of the garden and I read the scripture again.

When I approached Yah about it, was when He gave me this revelation. At first, I was with everyone else, never realizing until Yah gave me the Revelation that Adam was just as guilty as Eve at that very moment by the deception of the serpent. Either way, He could have stopped it. I started wondering if Adam was on the other side of the Garden of Eden somewhere chilling but he was not, and even if he was, he did not have to walk over to the forbidden tree with Eve. The following paragraph will explain. If Eve had taken fruit from the forbidden tree for herself and Adam and walked over to Adam to share the fruit with him. You would think that Adam had no clue thinking that Eve picked the fruit from any tree in the garden but the forbidden tree, unless the fruit from the forbidden tree had different fruit; however, scripture does not mention the difference. Therefore, the fruit must have been the same kind. It also came to mind that if she explained to Adam what the serpent told her with two pieces of fruit, one for him, and one for her, to eat together. Adam would still be at fault too because he could have snatched the fruit from her and tossed it to the ground.

If she did not explain it to him and just given him the fruit then he would not be guilty at all and I do not think that Yah would have punished Adam knowing that he was innocent. We know that Yah is all-knowing. He knew what took place before He met up with Adam later. Moreover, the scripture does not say that Eve took the fruit from the tree and found her husband in the garden to share with him, or walked across the garden to share with Adam.

Scripture clearly says that Eve saw that the tree was good for food, and it was delightful to look at, and a tree to be desired to make one wise and insightful, she took some of its fruit and ate it, and she also gave some to her husband with her, and he ate. There was no other man in the garden to consider that could have been her husband. Therefore, her husband could be no one else but Adam, so the quote "with her" could not mean anything else but literally with her, meaning right there beside her. I also believe this is why Yah called out to Adam when they were hidden because He was not innocent of the forbidden fruit. He told Adam the rule regarding the forbidden tree first. If Adam was truly innocent, I believe he would have said that I ate fruit that Eve gave me having no knowledge that it came from the forbidden tree. Therefore, they were both at the tree that Adam also knew better than to eat from and was guilty equally. The only difference is that Eve happened to bite the fruit first. It is wrong to put all the blame on Eve. I am about to dive into this to explain what I mean. I have **bold** the key points to back up what I am talking about. I will first start with the scriptures. And when the woman saw that the tree was good for food and that it was delightful to look at, and a tree to be desired to make one wise and insightful, she took some of its fruit and ate it; and she also gave some to her husband with her, and he ate.

I am reading from **Genesis Chapter 2 verses 15-17**; **Genesis Chapter 3 verses 6-7 (Amplified Bible)**

So Yah took the man [**He had made**] and settled him in the Garden of Eden to cultivate and keep it. And Yah commanded the man, saying, "You may freely (**unconditionally**) eat [**the fruit**] from every tree of the garden; but [**only**] from the tree of knowledge (**recognition**) of good and evil, you shall not eat, otherwise, on the day that you eat from it, you shall most certainly die [**because of your disobedience**]."

NOW REMEMBER, YAH SAID, "THE DAY YOU EAT FROM IT, YOU SHALL SURELY DIE." ADAM WAS PROBABLY THINKING **"IMMEDIATELY" (DROP DEAD INSTANTLY)**. I AM ABOUT TO EXPLAIN

WHY. PUT A BOOKMARK THERE AND GO TO **GENESIS Chapter 3 verses 6-7.** Remember I said I thought that Adam was way across the other part of the garden somewhere chilling? Let's read **Genesis Chapter 3 verses 6-7.**

And when the woman saw that the tree was good for food and that it was delightful to look at, and a tree to be desired to make one wise and insightful, she took some of its fruit and ate it; and she also gave some to her husband **<u>"WITH HER"</u>**, and he ate. Then the eyes of the two of them were opened [**that is, their awareness increased**], and they knew that they were naked, and they fastened fig leaves together and made themselves coverings.

The keywords are **<u>"WITH HER."</u>** Capitalize every letter, bold it, and underline it. Meaning he was right there standing beside her. **Therefore, ADAM was listening to the serpent** as well and should have told it to shut up but **Adam was interested just as much as Eve and was deceived**. In the beginning, before Eve, Yah told Adam first about the forbidden tree. However, Adam was sneaky with his, all he could hear from the voice of Yah when he first instructed him was that the day he eat of it, **HE WILL SURELY DIE!** Therefore, he most likely was thinking right away the same day. Therefore he waited for Eve to bite first to see if she would drop dead **immediately**. When he saw/thought it was safe to eat by not seeing her drop dead. Adam decided to eat too. Another reason you cannot blame Eve only is that when the serpent was talking to **"THEM"**, they were at **another location** in the garden of Eve.

This is where it really gets interesting because even if Adam was across another part of the Garden, they both had to walk to the forbidden tree so if Adam was so innocent why was he walking to the tree with Eve to try the fruit?

This was revealed to me coming from **Genesis Chapter 3 and verse 3, which** brings me to that conclusion. Except for the fruit from the **tree that is in the middle of the garden.** Yah said, 'You shall not eat from it nor **"<u>TOUCH IT</u>"**, otherwise you will die."Nevertheless, the serpent said to the woman, "You certainly will not die! (the serpent did not say right away or later) **"<u>TOUCH IT</u>,"** are the operative words. Underline, bold, and capitalize. If they knew not to **"<u>touch it</u>"** because it is possible to **die from doing so, much less eating its fruit**. Then they would not be anywhere near the tree in the first place, right? Therefore, they **BOTH** took a chance at the same time to walk over to that forbidden tree after the serpent lied to them **BOTH (in all caps).** I cannot say for sure, and of course, no one was there to witness Adam and Eve's conversation (**but Yah**). However, I would not be surprised if Adam told Eve to go ahead and try it first to see if she would drop dead **IMMEDIATELY**. When he realized that biting the fruit did not kill Eve, he decided to take a bite. Remember what scripture says, after she ate, she gave some to her husband **"WITH HER"** and he ate. Letting the reader know that he was not across another part of the garden somewhere chilling he was right there with her.

They were both in error at the same time. Stop putting all the blame on others. Somebody had to bite first and Eve happens to do so. Remember neither one had no business even being anywhere near the tree in the first place if Yah said it can kill you to even touch it. **Unless they would have said, "on the count of three" with the fruit to their lips to bite at the same time someone bit first and it happen to be Eve but I believe Adam was waiting to see what happens to Eve first**. The serpent deceived them both equally at the same time. Neither one should have been listening in the first place; they should have told the serpent to shut up because the serpent was out of place trying to get them to turn from what Yah said. However, they were both curious and wanted to do it. **NOT JUST EVE!** It was **ADAM and EVE equally in error** that started **the fall of all humankind. Again, it was not as if Adam was way across the other side of the garden somewhere. He was "WITH HER" being deceived just like Eve.** If he was across the garden somewhere else, I believe scripture would have said so.

I also want to emphasize the meaning of the word die

1. Separation from Yah. Adam and Eve were separated from Yah and lost direct contact with Him face-to-face.

2. The body ages daily to the point that one day the heart will stop pumping and the individual will die physically. From dust, the man came, and the physical body will return to dust. Before the sin of Adam & Eve that caused all humankind to fall. They were supposed to have lived eternally in the physical body, coming together to multiply the population on earth with offspring to worship. Yah.

3. Sin can also bring individuals to a physical death before their time if they do not repent this is found in **Ecclesiastes Chapter 7 verse 17** "Do not be excessively *or* willfully wicked and do not be a fool. Why should you die before your time?"

   Meaning does not willfully sin as sin becomes more wicked as you continue in it. One is not safe out of the will of Yah and willing to sin. His safety is not there to protect you. He will allow Satan to kill you before your time. Yah knows the end from the beginning and already knows if one would repent and turn their heart to Him, so sometimes He allows Satan to take a person out before their time.

4. One can die in their sins, never coming before Yah with a contrite heart, ask for forgiveness to be given grace and mercy for repenting, and start a relationship with Yah through Yahshua.

I have read ten translations of bibles that say the same. To those that want to say a different translation was recorded wrong regarding Adam being "WITH HER" Two translations did not say "with her"

(Amplified)
And when the woman saw that the tree was good for food and that it was delightful to look at, and a tree to be desired to make one wise and insightful, she took some of its fruit and ate it; and **she also gave some to her husband with her, and he ate**.

King James Version (KJV)
In addition, when the woman saw that the tree was good for

food and that it was pleasant to the eyes, and a tree to be desired to make one wise, she took of the fruit thereof, and did eat, and **gave unto her husband with her; and he did eat**.

The Living Bible (TLB) *
The woman was convinced. How lovely and fresh looking it was! In addition, it would make her so wise! Therefore, she ate some of the fruit and gave some to her husband, and he ate it too.

Modern English Bible (MEB)
When the woman saw that the tree was good for food, that it was pleasing to the eyes and a tree desirable to make one wise, she took of its fruit and ate; and she **gave it to her husband with her, and he ate**.

New American Bible (NAB)
The woman saw that the tree was good for food and pleasing to the eyes and the tree was desirable for gaining wisdom. So, she took some of its fruit and ate it; **and she also gave some to her husband, who was with her, and he ate it**.

New American Standard Bible (NASB)
When the woman saw that the tree was good for food, that it was a delight to the eyes, and that the tree was desirable to make *one* wise, she took some of its fruit and ate; **and she also gave *some* to her husband with her, and he ate.**

New English Translation (NASB)
When the woman saw that the tree produced fruit that was good for food, was attractive to the eye, and was desirable for making one wise, she took some of its fruit and ate it. **She also gave some of it to her husband who was with her, and he ate it**.

New International Version (NIV)
When the woman saw that the fruit of the tree was good for
food and pleasing to the eye, and desirable for gaining
wisdom, she took some and ate it. She **also gave some to
her husband, who was with her, and he ate it.**
New Life Version (NLV) *
The woman saw that the tree was good for food, pleasing to
the eyes, and could fill the desire of making one wise.
Therefore, she took its fruit and ate it. **She also gave some
to her husband, and he ate.**

The Cepher Bible says, "She ate and gave some to her
man, **with her. To sum this up.** When Adam and Eve
Both disobeyed Yah's instructions, they both wanted to
blame the other instead of coming clean with Yah
admitting their wrongdoing by disobeying Yah. Therefore,
when Adam blamed Eve, Yah told him what his
punishment would be since he wanted to say he listened to
Eve.

Again, if Eve traveled to Adam somewhere else in the
Garden to tell him what the serpent told her, he must have
agreed to try it out too and willing to walk to the forbidden
tree with her because scripture says that she took from the
tree ate and gave some to her husband, here it comes you'll
"WITH HER." Meaning he was standing right there with
her. Yah knows that Adam knew what he was doing all
along but he wanted to blame Eve so Yah told Adam what
his punishment would be as a man. When Eve blamed the
serpent Yah told Eve what her punishment would be as a
woman. Then Yah cursed the serpent and made him crawl
on his belly. Apparently, snakes used to be upright. Yah
saw the whole thing before it happened and He already
knew what was going to take place before it happened.

They were both equally wrong at the same time for disobeying Yah's instructions.

Therefore, they are **BOTH** the reason for the fall of all humanity from the beginning. **Not just Eve alone**. Yes, she bit first but Adam might have wanted to see her bite first to see if she would drop dead and Yah knew this too. Going back to what I said, somebody still had to bite first, unless they both had the fruit at their lips, and agreed to bite at the same time on the count of three or what number they chose.

For all we know, maybe if Adam and Eve would have both had come clean and admitted their sin and asked Yah to forgive them the punishment would not have been so severe or Yah might have given them another chance. However, humanity is suffering for it and we will never know. Nevertheless, I do thank Yah that He gave me the revelation that Eve should not be the one taking all the blame for the beginning of the fall of humanity because she bit the fruit first. When they were both guilty at the same time.

CHAPTER IX
THE TRUE NAME
OF OUR CREATOR

The concept that has spread globally that our creator "Yah" has many names is incorrect. The information I am presenting in this book is very easy to understand. I have created a chart to break down how people are confusing Yah's name with His attributes. I am also emphasizing how important it is to start calling the correct name of Yah and His son Yahshua in these last days. I also advise you to research for yourself. I truly believe most churches are out of order and coming apart because the leaders are not acknowledging the truth and aligning the scriptures in the bible to teach Yah's people correctly. Many church leaders are busy talking about material things and getting people's money. If the leaders are afraid of losing members in the church for telling the truth because they are afraid tithe and offerings will decrease and in fear they will no longer be able to live wealthy. That goes to show that the spirit operating in them is not of Yah.

That unclean spirit is controling those that love money more than they fear Yah. (**1 Timothy 6:10**).
They rather fear what the majority will think, and are afraid to lose money. Church leaders that are truly lead by the spirit of Yah will accept the truth and heed to it no matter the cost. They will be ok with becoming an outcast to other associate Pastors and possibly losing members of the church and becoming a loner because they fear Yah more than man and do not worship money. However, it is only a hand full of them. As long as he/she is in agreement with Yah and pleasing Him that is all what matters to them that truly love Yah, as it should be. Scripture says to fear the one that can destroy the body and soul (**and that can be only one individual, "Yah"**) (**Matthew 10:28**).
Yah is the only one that can order individuals to the lake of fire or to be with Him for eternity man or woman nor demons have that kind of power.

Yah holds us responsible to take what we have learned and apply it to our daily lives (Luke 12:48), to whom much is given much is required. Once we find out the truth, there is no more sacrifice for that sin. **Hebrews 10:26 (No more sacrifice of sins).** For if we go on willfully, *and* deliberately sinning after receiving the knowledge of the truth, there is no longer a sacrifice [**to atone**] for our sins [**that is… no further offering to anticipate**], but a kind of awful *and* terrifying expectation of [**divine**] judgment and THE FURY OF FIRE *and* BURNING WRATH WHICH WILL CONSUME THE ADVERSARIES [**those who put themselves in opposition to Yah**], **Timothy 6:10 (For the love of money)** For the love of money [**that is, the greedy desire for it and the willingness to gain it unethically**] is a root of all sorts of evil, and some by longing for it have wandered away from the faith and pierced themselves [**through and through**] with many sorrows.

Matthew 10:28 (Yah can kill the body and the soul) Do not be afraid of those who kill the body but cannot kill the soul, but rather be afraid of Him who can destroy both soul and body in hell.

Ezekiel 39:7
"I will make My holy name known among My people Israel and I will not let them profane My holy name anymore; and the nations will know that I am Yahuah (Yah), the Holy One of Israel. **Over 700 times the name Yahuah was replaced with Lord, God, and Jehovah. Psalm 68:4 (King James Version) is** the only scripture that did not remove the name of Yah and replaced it with "**Lord.**"

What is the meaning of **Hallelu**? The "Hebrew Bible," explains that it is a compound word, meaning, "**Praise joyously.**" Yah's name is shortened (**from Yahuah**), and when Yah is attached to "**Hallelu**" the compound word word turns into "**HalleluYah.**" Through the years of translations the "Y" was changed to "J" spelling it "jah." Therefore, when you say HalleluYah, you are giving praise and honor to Yah. Not God, which is considered a title, nor are you praising Lord or Jehovah.

Part of the compound word of Hallelu is Yah. You are saying "**praise Yah**." The full name of Yah is Yahuah. Most bible translations have replaced Yah with Lord, but not all. **See the scripture below *Psalm 68:4***
Sing unto Elohim, sing praises to his name. Praise Him that ride upon the heavens by his name JAH, and rejoice before him.

Many people think as long as they call on the title "God or Lord" as their creator and Jesus as their savior then the Father understands and will excuse it because He knows that they are addressing Him and His son. That is true until the individuals are taught the true name of the Almighty and His son name.

Many people figure they have been blessed and delivered while calling on those titles and pagan names, **"why change?"** Some figures "he must not mind and everyone is familiar with it anyway" "so **why stop?**" So many individuals feel this way and it is the most disrespectful, smack in the face, cuss to the face, and spit in the faces of Yah and Yahshua to even think that way.

I am talking to the ones that have learned Yah's true name and His son's true name but refuse to call them by their correct name. The following are three examples of what you are saying to Yah and Yahshua when you refuse to call them by their correct name.

    1.) When you call Yah and His son the names of titles and pagan names, it is the same as a woman calling out another man's name when she and her husband are making love.

2.) When you continue to call Yah and Yahshua titles and pagan names, and you know better, is like telling them to "hell with you'll proper name." "I am going to continue to call you names of titles and pagan names," "as I am familiar with it," as well as the majority whether it is offensive to you or not."

3.) To continue to call Yah and Yahshua pagan names and titles is placing them in a category with everyone else, but they should stand-alone. As Yah stated below in the scripture

Isaiah 42:8
"I am Yah, that is My **Name**; My glory I will not give to another, Nor My praise to carved idols (**gods and titles**). **For example,** the title god is used as many demeaning things, just to name a couple, "god-damn," and "**spirits of darkness**," those titles fall under gods and goddesses of mighty ones (**demons and pagan titles**) but Yah is the "Almighty." The title goddess is a female demon.

Remember Satan and demons have mighty powers too, but Yah and His son Yahshua are "ALMIGHTY OVER ALL POWERS." I recommend you get my book "**Divine Dictionary for Deliverance,**" which goes into more detail about demonic powers but Yah is overall. "Lord" is also a title; people call other people and objects lord. Yah and Yahshua are in a class by themselves, and should never be called these titles and pagan names; Yah and Yahshu have their own unique names.

YAH is most certainly the "Almighty" and the source of our salvation. He will give salvation to those who follow

Him completely through His son, and refuse to bow down or serve any Gods at all.

There is proof that the words El and Elohim were the very words the pagan Canaanites used for worshipping their own Gods. It is obvious from the study of the etymology of the Hebrew language, that the Children of Israel made the language of Canaan their own because of the snares of the Canaanites and their own disobedience to YAH. As we have seen the word El. It has been translated as God in many Scriptures, but it is of vital importance to know that this word has also been translated as power in three different Scriptures.

The words El, ElOHIM (GOD) and ADON, ADONAI (LORD) were slowly but surely, incorporated into the WORSHIP of the Israylites! Was Yah pleased with this worship? Well, as we have read in Revelation 12:9, the whole world is DECEIVED therefore, the worship of EL (God) and Elohim (Gods) is DECEPTION, as we find in:Elohim: God, god

Original Word: אֱלֹהִים
Part of Speech: Noun Masculine
Transliteration: elohim
Phonetic Spelling: (el-o-heem')
Definition: God, god
https://biblehub.com/hebrew/430.htm
Bible Strong's Hebrew 430 430. elohim Strong's Concordance elohim: **God, god** Original Word: אֱלֹהִים Part of Speech: Noun Masculine Transliteration: elohim Phonetic Spelling: (el-o-heem') Definition: **God, god** NAS Exhaustive Concordance Word.
This is the reason why I do not like to use Elohim when addressing Yah. It means God, mighty ones, but not

Almighty. Angels, satan and demons are considered mighty ones too but they are not the "ALMIGHTY."
Deuteronomy 11:16 Take heed to yourselves, that your heart be not deceived, and that you not turn aside, and serve gods, and worship them.

The word Elohim is the exact word that Yah CONDEMNS YOU for serving and worshipping, and is the exact word from which the English word God is translated.
The PAGAN word GOD comes from the word EL (singluar, GOD) or ELOHIM (plural-GODS) Yah is not plural. "He is self existing."

The Tetragrammaton: from the Greek words "Terpa" (Tetra) = "Four" (YHWH) + "ypauua" (gramma) = "LETTER" + "tov" – "THE": meaning "The four Letters," as in: The Transliterated Hebrew Name of God."

Exodus 3:14: And God said unto Moses, *I AM THAT I AM:* and he said, Thus shalt thou say unto the children of Israel, *I AM* hath sent me unto you.

https://www.academia.edu/40246583/In_Search_of_the_Sacred_Tetragrammaton_Name_of_God

**It is common to hear the names of "Yahweh" "Yah"
and "Jehovah" when attempting to describe the
"Almighty," of the Biblical
Israelites (Tribe of Juda so-called Hebrews). Where did
these names originate.**

Scripture Backup

Proverbs 28:9

He that turns away his ear from hearing the law, even his
prayer shall be an abomination.

Remember scripture says, "**My people perish for lack of
knowledge**" and for that reason, some really think that they
are calling on Yah when they say, God and Lord.
However, there is much deception in the world.
Nevertheless, Yah will wink at ignorance (**Acts 17:30**), but
when the truth is revealed you are no longer ignorant.
Moreover, there is no more sacrifice for sin (**Hebrews
10:26**) once you know the truth. Therefore, to find out His
true name and His son's true name and refuse to
acknowledge it is like spitting in Yah's face, telling Him I
do not respect you nor your son's **name**. It is like saying I
prefer to call you titles and the names of other entities
because you are no better than they are. Satan has even
made it so those that have removed the true names of Yah
and Yahshua from scripture to replace them with the title
"god or lord" by capitalizing the "G and L" to suggest they
are talking about the almighty and His son which is
blasphemous to me. To be identified as Yah and His son
and the little "g and l" as anyone or anything but Yah and
Yahshua. However, the fact remains the title "God and
Lord" is not His name, nor is Jesus His

son's name. Satan has deceived the whole world **(Revelations 12:9-10)**

Acts 17:29-30
Forasmuch then as we are the offspring of Yah, we ought not to think that the Yah-head is like unto gold, or silver, or stone, graven by art and man's
device. And the times of your ignorance Yah winked at, but now Yah commands all men everywhere to repent (**to turn from sin**)

Psalm 45:17
I will make your name be remembered in all generations; therefore, the people will praise *and* give you thanks forever and ever. (**This scripture is King David talking to Yah**).

Isaiah 52:6
Those who rule over them scream [**with teasing and ridicule of their salvation**]," declares Yah, "and My name is continually blasphemed all day long. **My people shall know My Name** *and* what it means. Therefore, on that day I am the One who is speaking, "Here I am," (**meaning when we call on his true name He will answer**). **Breakdown of Isaiah 52:6**, Yah is talking about how His people will suffer persecution in the last days, and if they refuse to call Him by His name He will not answer but those that do He will be there and say, "Here I am."

Malachi 1:11
For from the rising of the sun, even to its setting, My name shall be great among the nations.

In every place, incense is going to be offered to My name, and a pure grain offering; for My name shall be great among the nations," says Yah of hosts.

2 Corinthians 11:14-15
For such are false apostles, deceitful workers, transforming themselves into the apostles of Yahshua. In addition, no marvel, for Satan himself is transformed into an angel of light. Therefore, it is no great thing if his ministers also were transformed as the ministers of righteousness, whose end shall be according to their works.

Breakdown of 2 Corinthians 11:14-15. Many false leaders are in the church and deceiving the people to believe they are true men and women of Yah. However, Satan also disguises himself to people as friendly and wholesome, as a religious person, and deceives them. The majority of the time, Satan and demons that are sent to individuals do not come to people looking weird and evil but friendly. That is the reason we must test the spirit of the individual that comes to us in that way to make sure Satan has not sent them. Numerous times the so-called women and men of the cloth, as they say, are portraying themselves as pastors, Apostles, and Prophets but are ministers of Satan and in the end, the truth will come out.

For example, many leaders in the church have been exposed because of the sins they have committed. To name a few: molestation, rape, adultery, murder, stealing, is what the scripture means in the last verse that their end shall be according to their works will be exposed. I truly believe that the spirits of lust, envy, jealousy, and greed are invited into the church because of this error. To reiterate some do not really know the truth of Yah's name but many do and refuse to address Him and His son by their proper names. I believe churches are perishing because of it. When I say perishing. I am talking about the spiritual growth of the church and the bondage of the people. I am not talking about how much money coming through it. However, some Pastors and Leaders that know the truth are in more danger of **YAHUAH's** judgment because they turn their heads from the truth. They figure, "after all, it is a tradition as many say, and the norm to the average person." But that does not make it righteous according to the laws of Yah.I have even shared this truth with Pastor's of churches I used to attend when I was a Christian and none of them, but one I think actually repented. However, when the truth is revealed to someone and they do not abide there is no longer a sacrifice for sins. An individual perishes and becomes judged by Abba Father. This is a time to keep these particular scriptures in mind because the majority follows the familiar and norm.

When **YAHUAH** saved "only" one family in the city of Solemn & Gomorrah because of the wickedness in it, he saw that the one family was worth saving. The same for Noah and his family, they were the only ones found righteous in Yah's eyes.

The Savior's Name is Not Jesus
His Name is Yahshua

John 5:43
I have come in my Father's name, and ye receive me not: if another shall come in his own name, him ye will receive.

When Yahshua said he came in his father's name. He
literally came in Yah's name. The Hebrew language lets us
know Yah's name means "self-existent," and "shua" means
savior. Therefore, Yahshua's name means Yah saves. It is
that easy. When you accept Yahshua you receive Yah as
your savior if you receive another you receive him not and
you receive another. The majority is receiving Jesus,
Allah, God, Lord, Buddha, and so on.

Whatever name you accept as the one you worship that is
who you have received as the one to save you but no one
can save you but Yah through His son Yahshua. He is the
only one that has all power and is above every man,
woman, and demon. Nevertheless, if you are calling on
another's name as your Father and savior, Yah is not in it,
and there is nothing yahly about it. As you continue to call
on the name of a title or another entity and a title or pagan
name as your savior after the truth has been revealed that is
a dangerous thing. Do not be surprised if your prayers are
no longer answered. Nobody introduced me to Yah's
name. I am a witness to this Yah just stopped answering my
prayers and when I talked to Him in prayer about it; He told
me to go get a book I had ordered and it was packed away
two years ago (**at that time**) regarding the name of the

Creator and start reading it. I thought that the book was
referring to what I thought at one time as many others do
that Yah has many names. I found out that people confuse
His attributes with His name and so did I once upon a time
because that is what I was taught. The attributes includes
His name. Once I started calling Yah and Yahshua by their
correct names. My prayers were answered again.

Jesus Christ does not have anything to do with Abba Yah and His son.

CHRISTOS MITHRAS: means pure, sacred, good, and holy. (Roman meaning was inter-changeable: "good Mithras" or "holy Mithras"). But from whom?
Worshippers of Serapis were called "<u>Christians</u>".
Christianity - is a word that is <u>not</u> <u>found</u> in the Bible, nor in concordance. However, the title is used as a label for a religion supposedly founded by the Hebrew Messiah. Tradition has given the Hebrew Messiyah a Greek name. Nevertheless, He was only known as **"Yahshua"** during his days of walking on earth ministering and healing, which is a Hebrew name, not Greek. There is no letter "J" in the Hebrew or Greek alphabet.
The letter "J" is the last letter added to the alphabet. The J replaced the letter "I" in many instances. The letter "J" began as a typographical embellishment for the already existing "I."

With the introduction of lowercase letters to the Roman numeric system. The "J" was used to denote the conclusion of a series of ones— as in "xiij" for the number https://www.dictionary.com/e/j/

Scribes expressed the sound of both "I and J" interchangeably with the vowel and the consonant.

It was not until 1524 when Gian Giorgio Trissino, an Italian Renaissance grammarian known as the father of the letter "J," made a clear distinction between the two sounds. Trissino's contribution is important because once he distinguished the soft "J" sound, as in "jam" he was able to identify the Greek "Iesus" a translation of the Hebrew "Yeshua," as the Modern English "Jesus." Which became totally twisted and deleted the full meaning of Yahshua's name. Yahshua means, "Yah saves." Jesus means nothing of the sort.

Now, we all realize that Moses spoke neither English nor Modern Hebrew as the creation of these languages are thousands of years into the future, so we have to retrace our evolutionary language steps regarding the name that has come down to us as FOUR LETTERS that represent the Sacred Name of God. It is the Evolution of these letters representing the Sacred Name of God and the historical look at the evidence that may reveal what the original pronunciation might have been that is the subject of this research. Although I do believe that certain sounds are sacred, I really don't think it matters today what the pronunciation of the Sacred name is or was because the "thought form" is more important. To the Jewish world during his time 2000 years ago his name was "Yeshu'a" in Hebrew. To Christians today the name is *"Jesus"* and in Spanish it is spelled the same but pronounced "Hey-soos". The name Jesus comes from the Latin name *"Iesus"* which is a transliteration of the Greek name Ιησους (Iesous). However, as the New Testament was written in Greek, this Greek name was transliterated from the Hebrew name he was known by and how people called him by his Hebrew name יהושע / ישוע = "Yeshua" also spelled and pronounced "Yahshua", "Yehoshua" or as the English "Joshua". No one during his time called him by the Greek or English/Spanish name "Jesus" as we say today but in all cases. I believe it is the *intent* to call upon the Messiah in the language understood by the devotee at that or this particular time that is most important. The calling of someone's exact name to get their attention is indeed important and a biblical example is given in Mark 5:9. Jesus asks the evil spirits possessing the crazed man what its name was because he needed to know the name to properly cast them out. *And Jesus asked him, "What is thy name?" And he answered, saying, "My name is Legion (Λεγεων) for we are many."* Here we have the case where the name was important in a very unique but important situation. I take the position that it is the "thought form" and "intent" of calling upon a specific heavenly being regardless of what language you call upon 'him', 'her' or 'it' just as long as you are mindfully and visually engaged internally with the process of invocation and not just saying words in hopes that the Universe will respond like a Genie in a bottle!

With this reading and interpretation of Genesis 3:14, we learn a most fundamental and essential feature of the Biblical Exodus of the Hebrews and Israelites with the knowledge that "God" is not nameless and that this *"He"*, "she" or *"Androgynous"* God has a personal name to use when one wants to invoke the presence of this Most High God. We hear from many in the Christian world the names Yah, Yahweh and Jehovah but are these names a true representative of what was dictated to Moses? Moses spoke Egyptian as his first language and as a most powerful man who rose up from clan of a scribe to Viceroy of Kush (Nubia) then to Pharaoh before being overthrown. Moses no doubt spoke other languages of the local area. Before we go back more than 3000 years to the time of Moses to find *HOW* the Tetragrammaton may have been written, we must first go back a bit more than 2,600 years when the name of God was "unpronounceable" to the Israelites and Jews. Today, many Jews adhere to the centuries old tradition of not pronouncing the name of God referenced in Exodus 3:14. They instead use the names "Adonai" = "Lord" or "Elohim". Today it is also common for many Jews to simply say *'HaShem'*

<u>https://www.academia.edu/40246583/In_Search_of_the Sacred_Tetragrammaton_Name_of_God</u>

ENGLISH WORD "GOSPEL" The word "Gospel" is Old English. It's really 2 words crammed together: *GOD* + *SPEL* (Gott + spell). We have already seen that the Teutonic Celts worshipped the sun with the word "**GOD**", and it was a proper name.

The ***Encylopedia Americana*** (**1945 Edition**) says under the topic "GOD" Several words are derived from the root for "strength", EL:

The word "**ALLAH**" is derived from the Hebrew word, ELAH, and means "**the mighty one**" but not "**ALMIGHTY.**" The first word above is plural for EL: ELIM. The pronoun "ELOHIM" conveys the idea that Yahuah is the "Mighty One of oaths" but still does not point out **"ALMIGHTY"** and this is why I personally do not like to classify Yah as Elohim because it is defined as "mighty one" but not Almighty. Demons are considered mighty ones too but they are not Almighty. Just like Christ has nothing to do with our savior Yahshua. Although "**Christ**" in the Greek translation means anointed one, but anointed of whom? **Yahshua is the Messiyah anointed by Yah.**

ATTRIBUTES OF YAH'S NAME:

Many Confuse Yah's Attributes As the Name of Yah

El Shaddai	Yah Is Mighty
Yahuah Nissi	Yah Is My Banner
Yahuah Raah	Yah Is My Shepherd
Yahuah Rapha	Yah Heals
Yahuah Shammah	Yah Is There
Yahuah Tsidkenu	Yah Our Righteousness
Yahuah Meoddishkem	Yah Sanctifies You
El Olam	Everlasting Elohim
Qanna (Jealous)	Yah Is A Jealous Yah
Yahuah Yireh	Yah Provides
Yahuah Shalom	Yah is Peace
Yahuah Sabaoth	Yah Is Hosts

Y H>   I AM

H W>   HE (WHO)

H W H>   EXIST

YaHuWaH> I am He (who) Exists or I am He (who is) SELF EXISTENT

The titles of God and Lord; Christ, Jesus, and Jehovah are all Pagan and has nothing to do with Yah's name

**God= Gad a Babylonian deity (Strongs's Concordance)
H1408** meaning **Gawd** pronounced like **God**.

**Lord=BA'AL BA'AL Gad of Fortune (demon of
fortune)**

Jehovah= Is an artificial name (Meaning MISCHIEF)
and certainly has nothing to do with Yah's name as the
almighty or the name of His attributes. Mischief defines
harm, danger, disruption, and injury. **Hovah part of
Jehovah means RUIN and MISCHIEF in Hebrew
according to Strong's Concordance** #1943 *Hovah*,
**another form for 1942; RUIN:-MISCHIEF
Therefore, it is very offensive to call Yah Jehovah.**

Isaiah 65:11 (Amplified Bible)
"But you who abandon (**turn away from**) Yah, who
forget *and* ignore My holy mountain (**Zion**), who set a
table for Gad [**the Babylonian god of fortune**]. And who
fills a jug of mixed wine for Meni [**the god of fate**]

Exodus 20:7
"You shall not take the name of Yah your Elohim in vain
[**that is, irreverently, in false affirmations or in ways
that impugn the character of Yah**]; for Yah will not hold
anyone guiltless *nor* leave unpunished the one who takes
His name in vain [**disregarding its reverence and its
power**].

At the beginning of the reign of Jehoiakim the son of
Josiah, king of Judah, this word came from Yahuah,
saying, "Thus says Yah, 'Stand in the court of

Yahuah's house [**Jeremiah**]. Speak to all [**the people of**] the cities of Judah who have come to worship in Yah's house all the words that I have commanded you to speak to them. **Do not omit a word!** It may be that they will listen and everyone will turn from his wickedness, so that I may relent *and* reverse [**My decision concerning**] the disaster which I am planning to do to them because of their malevolent deeds.' And you will say to them 'thus says Yah, "If you will not listen to Me and obey My law which I have set before you, and listen *and* follow [**carefully**] the words of My servants the prophets, whom I have been sending to you repeatedly—though you have not listened then I will make this house [**the temple**] like Shiloh." I will make this city [**subject to**] the curse of all nations of the earth,

THE LETTER "J" WAS NEVER A PART OF THE HEBREW OR GREEK ALPHABET

Yahshua's name could never have been Jesus over two-thousand years ago because the letter "J" is no more than five hundred years old. Again, Yah will wink when he knows you do not know any better but once you know the truth you are responsible for using the knowledge that you know. According to the alphabet chart, there was never the letter "J" used in Hebrew, Greek, or Latin. Yah answered your prayers when calling on those titles and pagan names because He knew you did not know any better but He saw your faith that got your prayers answered.

However, now that you know the truth He expects you to call Him and His son by their proper name. If you still try to use those pagan names and titles when petitioning Yah through His son Yahshua. **YOUR PRAYERS WILL NOT BE HEARD!!!** I am a witness to that. Therefore, I advise you to start calling Him and His son by their correct name because now you are equipped with the knowledge of the truth.

POEM

**"WHAT HAPPENED
TO OUR CREATOR'S NAME?"**

VIGOROUS WITH LIES DISPLAYED AS TRUTH, WHEN WILL YOU COME TO A TRUCE?

THOSE THAT CALL THEMSELVES CHILDREN OF THE CREATOR

HOW CAN YOU SAY YOU LOVE HIM WHEN YOU DO NOT RESPECT HIS NAME?

HOW DO YOU EXPECT HIM TO PROTECT YOU WHEN YOU CALL THE WRONG NAME?

NOT TO BE CARNAL BUT TO CALL OUT A TITLE OR PAGAN NAME TAKING THE PLACE OF HIS,

IS LIKE A MAN MAKING LOVE TO HIS WIFE AND SHE CALLS OUT ANOTHER MAN'S NAME

JUST LIKE PARENTS GIVING THEIR NEWBORN CHILD A MEANINGFUL NAME,

BUT THE CHILD DOESN'T LIKE IT BECAUSE IT'S NOT POPULAR HE/SHE GROWS UP, CHANGE THEIR NAME, BREAK THEIR PARENTS' HEART, AND PUT THEM TO SHAME TO NOT RESPECT OUR CREATOR'S NAME, I BELIEVE HE FEELS THE SAME, THOSE THAT DID NOT KNOW ANY BETTER YAH EXCUSED, BUT NOW THAT YOU KNOW THE TRUTH WHAT WILL YOU DO? HOW IS IT THAT YOU FIND OUT THE TRUTH ABOUT THESE PAGAN NAMES REFUSING TO TURN AND REPENT, AND ARE DETERMINED TO CALL ON THE NAMES OF GOD, LORD, AND JESUS THAT ARE IN VAIN?

THOSE NAMES HAVE NOTHING TO DO WITH OUR CREATOR AND HIS PRECIOUS SON'S NAME, YAH OUR CREATOR, AND YAHSHUA HIS SON, BOTH ARE POWERFUL NAMES "ABOVE ALL," FATHER YAH IS MERCIFUL AND FULL OF GRACE HE OFTEN SENDS, BUT ONCE THE TRUTH IS REVEALED THERE IS NO MORE SACRIFICE OF SINS (**Hebrew 10:26**).

I LOVE YOU YAH THROUGH YOUR SON YAHSHUA WHO DIED FOR ME ON GOLGOTHA, NAILED TO A STAKE SO THAT I CAN ESCAPE THE HORRORS OF THE PAGAN MESS IN "THE UNITED STATES"

LETTER CHART

Latin	Hebrew	Aramaic			Greek	
A alef	𐤀	א	1	ox	alpha	A
B beth	𐤁	ב	2	house	beta	B
G gimel	𐤂	ג	3	camel	gamma	Γ
D daleth	𐤃	ד	4	door	delta	Δ
H hay	𐤄	ה	5	window	hoi	H
U uau	𐤅	ו	6	hook	upsilon	Y
Z zayin	𐤆	ז	7	weapon	zeta	Z
CH heth	𐤇	ח	8	fence	(h)eta	H
T teth	𐤈	ט	9	winding	theta	Θ
Y yod	𐤉	י	10	hand	iota	I
K kaph	𐤊	כ	20	bent hand	kappa	K
L lamed	𐤋	ל	30	goad	lambda	Λ
M mem	𐤌	מ	40	water	mu	M
N nun	𐤍	נ	50	fish	nu	N
S samek	𐤎	ס	60	prop	xei	Ξ
E/A ayin	𐤏	ע	70	eye	omega	Ω
P pe	𐤐	פ	80	mouth	pei	Π
TS tsadee	𐤑	צ	90	hook	zeta	Z
Q koph	𐤒	ק	100	needle eye	chi	X
R resh	𐤓	ר	200	head	rho	P
SH shin	𐤔	ש	300	tooth	sigma	Σ
T tau	𐤕	ת	400	mark	tau	T

When placed in their combined Conjunctive / Compound form, they merge in order to make :

1)   יה = Y H
2)   הו = H W   Y H W H
3)   הוה = H W H

The FULLNESS of HIS NAME, in the terms of those FOUR LETTERS.

$$
\begin{array}{rcl}
יה & = & Y H \quad : \text{I AM} \\
הו & = & H W \quad : \text{HE (who)} \\
הוה & = & H W H : \text{EXISTS}
\end{array}
$$

YaHuWaH

I AM HE (who) EXISTS or I AM HE (who is) SELF EXISTANT

Hebrew Translations

YHWH/Yah (Creator)

Yahshua/Son of Yahuah

Torah/Law Written Scriptures

Shabbat/Sabbath **(Day of Rest)**

"Set-Apart Day"

Abba/Father **(Creator)**

Ruach/Spirit

Rauch haKodesh (Set-Apart Spirit)

Avraham/Abraham

Yisreal/Israel

Moshe/Moses

Moshiach/Messiah

Yithak/Isaac

Yaakov/Jacob

Shaul/Paul

Yoseph/Joseph

Beit/House

Baytim/Houses

Zera/Seed

Yahrushalayim/Jerusalem

Emunah/Faith

Kidushim/Saints

Shomer/Keep the Commandments of **YHWH**

Yirmeyahu/Jeremiah

Ivrim/Hebrews

Ephsiyah/Ephesians

Kepha/Peter

Alef/2

Luqas/Luke

Yochanan/John

Qolesayah/Colossians

Talmid/Students (modernly called disciples)

"Halacha/Walk" In

Yahshua's Foot Steps

Timtheous/Timothy

Beresheeth/Genesis

Romiyah/Roman

Gilyahna/Revelations

Yahuda/Juda

Mattityahu/Matthew

Yehchezkel/Ezekiel

Tehillim/Psalms/**condemn/expose darkness"**

Notsrim/Nazarenes

Chayim/Life

Yahudim/Hebrew

Hazeh/World

Zecharyah/Zechariah

Shemoth/Exodus

Devirim/Deuteronomy

Sholomo/Solomon

Ezrah/Ezra

Nechemyah/Nehemiah

Aliyah/Return

Phylypsiyah/Philippians

Ahava/Love

Neviim/Prophet

Greco/Roman

Ketuvim/Writings

Besarot/Good News

Galuyah/Galatians

REFERENCES
&
RECOMMENDATIONS

Other books written by me concerning History are:

"Who Are the True Chosen People of Yah"

"Divine Dictionary for Deliverance"

"Tears for My Sisters"; "What's Behind Secular Music"

Type my full name in "Google Search" and all of my books will populate.

Please send an email to tearsformysisters3588@gmail.com for feedback.

Bible used for Scriptures: Amplified Bible

Some Information gathered regarding Yah's name
https://www.academia.edu/40246583/In_Search_of_the_Sacred_Tetragrammaton_Name_of_God

The Breakdown of Elohim and Adonai comes from:
The New UNGER'S Bible Dictionary (**Merrill F. Unger**)

Hebrew & Greek translations from Strong's Concordance

Poem: "What Happened To Our Creator's Name"
written by: **Tonida J. Cooper**